The Lord of Possibilities
Miracles of Jesus

by LeRoy Lawson

Illustrated by James Seward

A division of STANDARD PUBLISHING
Cincinnati, Ohio
39995

Library of Congress Catalog Card No. 79-66502
ISBN: 0-87239-376-3

© 1980
The STANDARD PUBLISHING COMPANY, Cincinnati, Ohio.
Division of STANDEX INTERNATIONAL CORPORATION.
Printed in U.S.A.

Contents

Introduction

"With God nothing will be impossible" is the theme that holds all the chapters of this book together. To study Christ's miracles is to enter with awe into a world in which God is in charge, with the winds and waves and senses and powers below, and the principalities and authorities above all subject to His command. To a twentieth-century reader, hardened by his worship of technology and proud of his sophisticated skepticism, Christ's world might seem to be a land of make-believe, filled with strange and wondrous happenings too incredible to accept.

To a believer in God, however, the Gospel documents speak of the real world. There God hears and He answers prayer. There every human petitioner receives love from the Father of all. In God's world all the possibilities of the universe lie at the disposal of the believer who will but ask without doubting. There it is possible to walk on water, even when the wind is blowing; to transcend the boundaries of time to catch a glimpse of Christ with Moses and Elijah; and to roll back the stone at the door of a tomb in order to set free a body that death cannot hold.

To enter God's wonderful world of miracles is to realize, first, that His world is now and here. If the Holy Spirit has come, as Jesus promised, then the power that healed the blind and calmed the storms is present. Those who believe in God can live by faith in that power, a faith that is more than a feeling in the soul. It is an entrance into God's real world, where more is possible than our gadget-glutted society can dream of.

This study of miracles, then, becomes inescapably a study of faith—not of faith as an object of research, but of our faith—that is, my faith and yours. It is a personal adventure, one which will not allow us to remain academic or aloof: we shall find our whole selves involved, responding to Christ's invitation to walk in faith as Peter stepped onto the water in response to Christ's "Come."

Our response will be intellectual, of course. We shall read the reports of Christ's miracles with mental alertness. Every miracle will elicit questions: How did it happen? Why? Since we know that Jesus refused to pander to the crowd's expectations and perform as a magician or entertainer, why has He changed the water into wine, why has He cursed the fig tree, why? We cannot stop there, either. In every instance we shall also have to ask, "What have You to do with me, Jesus?" We cannot be comfortable unless we know what His healing of the man beside the pool has to do with our own chronic complaints of loneliness and sickness. So we shall be forced to respond to the miracles intellectually.

Our probings will lead us further, however. Our responses will be devotional. As the disciples, awed by Christ's display of power, worshiped Him, so we shall find ourselves almost involuntarily calling Him Lord. We cannot but recognize that He who can turn water into wine is also the Lord of the natural fermentation process. He who can stop the winds is the designer of all winds and waves. He who can summon Moses and Elijah for a mountaintop conference with Jesus is He who was and is and always will be, beyond the clutches of time and space, infinite against our finitude. He who is Lord of all will become Lord of you and Lord of me.

Intellectual curiosity leads to devotion, which leads to service. We cannot call Him Lord, Lord, and fail to serve Him. Faith is, finally, the service of trust; it is adventuring forward in activities that praise Him and serve His purposes. It is our own experiment with the impossible.

A saintly Christian explained miraculous faith in this simple way: "If God wants to perform a small miracle, He places us in difficult circumstances; if He wants to perform a mighty miracle He places us in impossible circumstances." There was no doubt in this saint's mind that God is still doing the impossible. Through His Spirit God continues to reveal himself to His people and to work His purposes in ways that baffle the skeptic. What is so exciting is that He works His difficult or impossible wonders through us, letting us participate in His powerful deeds. That is the kind of God Christ shows to us in His miracles.

In the following chapters, then, you will be learning of God's power and of your own possibilities. You already understand, of course, that my book is not the final word on what any Scriptural passage means. I do not specifically delimit the concept of miracle by any propositional definition. I am so convinced of the power of God to do whatever He wants to that I am suspicious of any human endeavor to define (that is, to draw limits around His power). My purpose is to present New Testament truth as clearly as I can perceive and describe it. It is simply my understanding. Yours may be better. When you disagree with me, you may very well be right; but when you disagree with the Scriptures—well, you'd better read them again! May you open yourself to be used by the God with whom nothing is impossible.

—LeRoy Lawson

Unless otherwise identified, Scripture quotations are from the *Revised Standard Version*.

Chapter 1

With God Nothing Is Impossible

(Luke 1:26-38)

I needed to prepare this study of Christ's miracles because I too frequently hear myself saying, "That's impossible." That little statement limits personal growth; it short-circuits the flow of God's power through us. Having already announced that we cannot do something, we have no trouble proving ourselves correct.

A few years ago we were remodeling our house in Tennessee. My wife, Joy, was the decorator and her father the contractor. From time to time Joy would talk over her plans with me—she had some really outrageous ones. She would carefully explain what she wanted to do and I would say, "You can't do that; that's impossible." So being the good loyal wife she is, she would appeal over my head to her father. She would explain the idea to him and he would invariably say, "That's no problem—it'll be easy." So she would design it and he would do it and I would go to the bank and pay for it. As I watched them transform our house I realized that it was fairly easy. I had called it impossible because I didn't know what I was talking about, and didn't appreciate their abilities and power.

We often come to the Scriptures with exactly that same mind set. We say, "But that's impossible," about some of Christ's miracles. The Gospel, however, asserts even more emphatically, *"With God **nothing** will be impossible."* That's the message of the miracles.

7

Jesus' life began among impossibilities, or at least improbabilities, if you please. This brief passage begins with the appearance of a supernatural messenger, an angel. Now, we know there are no such things as angels; they're really just figments of religious fanaticism's imagination. So some will tell us, because they have already excluded them, having decided that they cannot exist because they are not like us, and anything that is not like us or that we cannot understand cannot exist.

Another improbability is this pure girl in a wicked town. Nazareth, not a very large city, was on a major trade route in Palestine. It was the stop-over place for Roman soldiers and for traders. You know that stopover places for soldiers and traders are never innocent cities; and there were many indeed, male and female, who served the various desires of these men. Nazareth's reputation was so sordid that Nathanael later was only asking of Jesus' hometown what anyone else would have asked, "Can anything good come out of Nazareth?"

Of course, it is not impossible to find a pure girl in a wicked city—but it's rather rare.

And, of course, at the heart of the story is the impossibility of conception without sexual intercourse. The natural processes of biology are being bypassed. For a long time even some Bible scholars have held that this couldn't have happened. Now they aren't quite so sure, because genetic experiments have widely expanded the limits of biological possibilities. But for generations we were told it was impossible. That's why the theory arose that Jesus was not the Son of God but the illegitimate son of a Roman soldier whose desires Mary satisfied.

Another impossibility: Elizabeth, an old woman far past the age of child-bearing, now is going to have a baby, the angel says, as evidence of God working among them.

But the most difficult impossibility to receive is the assertion that God himself will visit this planet, that this promised baby is God's way of appearing upon the earth, that He will be called great, the Son of the most High. The Lord God will give Him the throne of David His father, the angel pledges, and He will reign over the house of Jacob forever and ever. Something dramatic and divine is happening here.

We usually don't make too much of the virgin birth, for the very good reason that the other major world religions claim miraculous births for their founders, too. Christianity does not rest upon the miracles associated with the birth of Christ, but upon the miracle of Christ's resurrection from the dead. That event is unique in all history and fundamental to the Christian faith. While the miraculous birth of Christ is less important than His resurrection, however, it seems strange that some believers categorically deny the virgin birth by simply saying God couldn't or wouldn't do it, or that it cannot happen because it violates biology. Who made biology preeminent? Is our proof of the existence of God dependent upon biology?

What we have here at the start of Christ's ministry is the assertion that *with God nothing is impossible*. It may seem impossible to our categories and systems, but the Bible asserts time and time again that God can do our impossibilities. We err grievously if with our limited, fallible minds we deny God's power. God has the ability to make Christ great, to grant Him the throne of David, to sustain Him forever and ever upon that throne. God surely has the power to fulfill the promises recorded in the Old Testament. He had assured Abraham and Isaac and Jacob that He would be their God forever. He kept His promise. If God had the power to place David upon the throne and promise him a Descendant who would rule forever, surely God has the power to announce to Mary that the time has come now for Him to keep His word. This is exactly what Paul says that He did: *"But when the time had fully come, God sent forth his Son, born of woman, born under the law, to re-*

9

deem those who were under the law" (Galatians 4:4). God kept His promise. It was possible for Him to do so.

Philippians says that Christ didn't count His pre-earthly equality with God a thing to be grasped, but He emptied himself and took the form of a servant—a human form—and came to earth. The message of the New Testament is that in Christ and through Christ we find all of God that we can comprehend. All of God cannot be limited to human form, of course, but all that we can comprehend we can see at work in Christ.

Does it seem impossible that God would want to communicate with us and would choose a way that He knows we could understand?

I don't know how you are, but when I'm talking to a little child, I instinctively go down on my knees to look into the child's eyes. (Maybe it is because I so often look up to others that I'm sympathetic with the child.) I also change my vocabulary so that I will be understood by the child. You do the same thing. You're simply trying to communicate.

Doesn't it seem conceivable that God so loved the created world that He wanted to communicate with it? Not only is it possible, it makes good sense, and it is sad when our categories insist that it cannot be done. Tennyson thought about this for a long time, and he finally decided that it may be our systems of thought that are wrong and not God.

Our little systems have their day,
They have their day and cease to be,
They are but broken lights of thee,
And thou, O Lord, art more than they.

When our thought systems say to the powerful God, "You can't do that because our minds won't allow it," we are somewhat like that old farmer who came to the city and for the first time in his life visited the zoo. He was fascinated by the animals. He had long known about cows and horses and pigeons and pigs, but in the zoo he met some strange new ones.

The one that really caught his attention was the giraffe. He stood and looked long at the stretched-out animal. Finally the fellow with him said, "What do you think of the giraffe?" The old man turned around, spit, and said, "Phooey. They ain't no such animal."

With that statement he denied the existence of the giraffe. So some say, "They ain't no miracles. They ain't no virgin birth, either." They won't allow it, trapped in a vocabulary and thought system that will not admit that God may accomplish possibilities beyond our imagination. In the birth of Christ and in the following miracles we're going to study, the God of possibility stretches our imagination to what can be.

Remember: With God nothing is impossible. Nothing. The birth of Christ is history. Something dramatic happened in Bethlehem when Christ came to earth. But the miracle continues, for Christ, Scripture tell us, is constantly coming to earth in the power of His Spirit and working within His church.

You may become a little impatient with me as I repeat this theme throughout the book, but I cannot say other than what the miracles themselves teach. If it was a miracle that Christ came, and that He comes by the power of His Spirit and works among us, then, so help me, friends, the church has God's miraculous power. We are limited only by our lack of faith in that power. For too long we've been trapped by what we know, and we've been afraid to venture forth to what we don't know, therefore effectively denying the power of God to do the impossible.

It is also interesting to note that Christ comes in the future. At the close of the age, the Scriptures tell us, the Christ who came at Bethlehem and who comes constantly to the church in His Spirit will come one day and wrap it all up. That's the God that we have, and He is our hope. Nothing else, in fact, is our hope.

In the early part of the nineteenth century, in the midst of England's struggle against the French emperor Napoleon, the United States Secretary of State,

Thomas Pickering, proposed a toast to Britain, calling that nation "the world's last hope—Britain's fast anchored isle."

During World War II, Winston Churchill made a little speech about Britain at the Lord Mayor's dinner in London. He said:

> Here we are and here we stand, a veritable rock of salvation in this drifting world . . . British and American forces continue to prosper in the Mediterranean. The whole event will be . . . a new hope for the whole world.

Now where is Britain, the world's last hope? Why, it's but a shadow of its former self, dependent upon other countries, with an economy in desperate shape. Britain is but a faint reminder of the glory that once was the Commonwealth. What about America, confused and floundering as a world leader? Is this our last hope? Our rock of salvation? Of course not. Our Salvation was promised long ago by the prophet Isaiah: *"For to us a child is born, to us a son is given; and the government will be upon his shoulder, and his name will be called 'Wonderful Counselor, Mighty God, Everlasting Father, Prince of Peace' "* (Isaiah 9:6).

Our hope is not in earthly institutions or bureaucracies or governments. They've let us down. We hope in a God who specializes in the impossible, who can do what no other can do. So Paul could say, *"I can do all things—**all things**—in him who strengthens me"* (Philippians 4:13).

And Christ would say to us, *"Ask, and it will be given you; seek, and you will find; knock, and it will be opened to you"* (Matthew 7:7).

Study Mark 9, the account of the father of a pitiful son given to such awful fits that they would throw him into fire or water. The father had searched everywhere for help for the little boy and he couldn't get any. He came to Jesus' disciples and they didn't know what to do. So finally he turned to Jesus and he begged, *"If you can do anything, have pity on us and* help us." Jesus said to him, "*If you can! All things are possible to him who believes.*" And Jesus healed the boy.

On another occasion Jesus talked of that little grain, the mustard seed. He said that if you have just that little bit of faith, even mountains would move for you and "*nothing,*" He said, "*will be impossible to you*" (Matthew 17:20). Yet, as you are reading these sentences you are probably thinking, "He can't really be serious. Life just doesn't work this way." You may be right—but then, you may also be wrong. You say it can't be true. God says it can be. Whom should I believe? Is my faith in you or in God?

These studies of the miracles will stretch our imaginations to think of possibilities to replace the impossibilities that have dominated and reduced our lives.

Last night I sat in the family room with Joy and the children. The television set was on. Into our room came various tones and intensities of colored light. How did they get there? Had my great-grandfather been with us he would have said, "That's a miracle." I went into the kitchen to get a drink of water. I just turned a tap and the water came. Not too many centuries ago that would have been a miracle. We heated up a little something in Joy's microwave oven. We put the food in and, only minutes later, when we took it out the food was hot but the oven and the plate were cool. To my grandmother that would have been a miracle. When we were ready to go to bed we turned off the light, simply flipped a switch and the lights went off. We could flip it again and they would come back on. Not very long ago that, too, would have seemed miraculous.

I came to work this morning in my very own horseless carriage. Who would have thought, one hundred years ago, that my carriage could have run without a horse?

We have a new little box by the front door of our church. If the doors are locked, you can push a little button and a voice will come from somewhere asking who's there. A voice out of nowhere at the push of a button. Not so long ago that would have been regarded as a miracle.

I sit at my desk and I talk into a little microphone and in another room a secretary takes down what I have just said. The phone on my desk rings. I have only to lift the receiver to talk to somebody miles away.

And you tell me we can't do the impossible! How did we get all these modern conveniences? Oh, you can explain them by physical laws. That's quite all right. I'll grant you that. But how did we get them? I'll tell you how we got them. We got them because a few years ago some people were doing a little thinking. They were not bound by what other people told them was possible. They dared to dream unthinkable dreams, to imagine the impossible. Do you realize that it has been in the Christian civilization that these miracles first occurred? Do you think that there might be some relation between belief in a God who can do the impossible and people who seek to imitate Him by also doing the impossible?

I believe in the Lord of possibilities.

Chapter 2

The Wedding Miracle

(John 2:1-11)

With this and the other miracles we shall be studying, a nagging question persists: How did Jesus do it? Having been brought up in a so-called scientific age we stumble over the details of a story like this one. How was it possible to change water to wine? We want to know.

John doesn't tell us. He doesn't even raise the issue. He believes in Christ and is convinced that if Christ wants to make wine out of water, He can. He's not interested in how, but in why Jesus does it.

I wish I were more like John, but I'm not. *How* is important to me. I'm the kind of person who is so bothered by how that I can't stand a magician's act. Nothing frustrates me so much as my inability to figure out how he is deceiving me. I know that skulduggery is going on and that the magician is making a fool out of me. I just don't know how.

John doesn't stumble on the how. He is concerned about the larger question of why. He says that Jesus performed this miracle at the wedding feast in Cana to demonstrate His "Heaven-sent power" *(The Living Bible)*. John includes this event in his book to help us believe in Jesus (John 20:30, 31).

So while we read the story and wonder how the wine got there, John concentrates on Jesus and hopes that because of his story we will be able to believe in the Master.

By comparison with some of Jesus' later signs, this one seems to be almost understated. Jesus does

15

not attract any attention to himself. I appreciate that. Some of the best miracles are not those that make headlines but the quiet events in the lives of persons who are being changed by Christ—quietly healed, radically but quietly converted, an undramatic change of attitude that changes a life.

As John draws our attention to Jesus' power he also draws our attention to His popularity. Some people who think of religion as that which takes the fun out of life will have trouble picturing Jesus as the life of the party. But He went to this wedding as an invited guest, and a wedding celebration was a supremely joyous occasion. Jewish parents would save for years in order to host an extravagant party for their son and his bride. For a week there would be eating and drinking and gaiety. Jesus, who obviously loved life, was not out of place there.

The Messiah did not come to spoil the party. He defended himself on one occasion, in fact, because He was being criticized for being too full of fun. "You've criticized John the Baptist because John comes neither eating nor drinking and you reject him because of that. Now you criticize me because I have come eating and drinking—you call me a glutton and drunkard" (Matthew 11:16-19). They thought His behavior quite unbecoming a religious leader. It's interesting, in fact, to note that early in His ministry the people who knew Jesus best didn't think of Him as being particularly religious. They knew what it meant to be religious, and by their definition of a religious person Jesus didn't fit.

They knew who was religious—not Jesus, but His brother, James. He obeyed the strictest rules of the Jews; he made quite a name for himself in religious circles for his piety and his ascetic life. If anybody had selected one of Joseph's sons as the religious brother, he wouldn't have mentioned Jesus, but James.

There is a bit of a danger that long-time Christians might no longer see Jesus as He really is. I'm convinced, for example, that we forget about His miracle-working power. We know Him too well. We've become such good buddies with Him we think of Him as too much like us to be able to do what we cannot do. That's one danger. Another is to make Him such an awesome object of religious devotion that we can't imagine Him laughing or having a good time at a party, a popular guest among His friends at the wedding celebration.

When the film, *Jesus of Nazareth,* was on TV I realized how rigid my image of Jesus had become. I liked the film. I disagreed with a lot of it, thinking some of the interpretations to be dead wrong, but some of the errors I thought I spotted weren't errors at all. After rethinking the Biblical account I would realize that the film's interpretation was probably closer to the truth than my own prejudice was. I was surprised to discover how encrusted my thinking about Jesus had become. It was good for me to see that film, particularly to be reminded of the way that people gravitated toward Jesus. He was popular. He was the kind of person you invite to a party.

His popularity stems from His love for common people. How unusual that was among the leaders of the ancient world. Plato, for example, thought it right to despise men who had to work for a living and couldn't devote all their energy to friendship and the affairs of state. Aristotle taught that all forms of labor which require physical strength are degrading to a free man. Cicero said a mechanical occupation is demeaning and a workshop incompatible with anything noble. To work with your hands, he said, demeans a man. There are times at my house when I find it very helpful to quote Cicero. My wife, not knowing much about ancient philosophers but a lot more about Christ, however, quotes some of His teachings to me and I always lose. She emphasizes the fact that Jesus was a carpenter; He worked with His hands. The Bible never suggests that there is anything demeaning about working with your hands. Instead, it elevates the life of the worker and considers it noble.

So we find Jesus in a wedding of common people, most of whom worked with their hands. If this had been a wedding of a famous, important person in the community, John would have told us so. I rather think that these were just folks, that this was an ordinary wedding, and that Jesus was invited because of His love for common people. It is His presence that dignifies the occasion and makes it uncommon. He bestows honor on all who are there.

Helmut Thieleke tells a touching story about this kind of bestowed dignity. When he was a schoolboy, he and some of his friends developed a real dislike for another boy. He was a pusher, a bully. Thieleke and his friends decided to gang up on him and give him a real thrashing, bringing him down a notch or two. But when they were just about ready to do that, Thieleke one morning was going to school at the same time that this boy's father was bringing him to school. The father was respected as the most distinguished man in town, and when he said good-bye to his son, he put his hand on the boy's head and patted his cheek, and as he walked off the father waved to him until he was out of sight. Thieleke said he could never look at that bully the same way again. He realized the boy really hadn't changed. He was the same pusher, all right, but he was also a pusher who was loved by a very distinguished man. He said this splendor of another's love lay around him.[1]

I know how that works. When I was in high school our principal was Student Enemy Number One. We didn't like that guy and in some respects perhaps he deserved our dislike. We enjoyed getting together and talking about what we thought of the principal. But something always spoiled our hate sessions. The problem was that the man had married a wonderful wife. She worked at the school, too. She liked the students; she was unfailingly kind to us. She was a good woman, and she loved her husband.

Thus, whenever we were right in the midst of a really good hate-the-principal session, somebody would mention his wife. That took all the sting out of our talk. We were forced to think a little better of the man because he was loved by such a good woman. She gave him a kind of borrowed dignity.

This is what Jesus does for common people. We don't think so highly of ourselves. We know who we are, we know our faults. Nobody has to preach about sin to us; we are aware of our sinfulness. But we also know that somebody very distinguished loves us. We, too, enjoy a kind of borrowed dignity.

Jesus walked with common people, went to their parties, enjoyed their weddings and made them feel a little taller. He loved them and was always ready to help them.

That is why Mary turned so naturally to Him for help. She was undoubtedly accustomed to His assistance. You will recall that no mention is made of Joseph after Jesus became an adult. He must have died earlier, leaving Mary a widow with a growing family. Jesus was the firstborn Son, so He became the head of the house. For years, then, Mary had been relying on Jesus. Jesus may very well have had to remain at home until He was thirty to take care of His mother and the children until the younger brothers were old enough to take over for Him. Then He was free to begin His ministry. We aren't certain that this speculation is accurate, of course, but we can be certain of His eagerness to help her and others who needed Him.

So Mary turned to Him automatically and He helped. I'm impressed that He let others help, too. He didn't do it alone. Instead of snapping His fingers to change the water to wine, He asked the servants to fill the jugs. It is the Lord's way to let His followers participate in His ministry. What that does for us! You can hear those servants boasting for the rest of their lives of that miraculous day and their part in the drama.

My father did something like that for me as a boy, and I'll be grateful to him all my life. Dad was a grocer and early in my life—altogether too early I thought at the time—he put me to work in his grocery store. I'm very proud of my training and of his patience with me. Some of my most vivid memories of those days are of the things that I broke or spilled, like the watermelon that rolled off the scales after I had weighed it, or the broken jar of molasses that took forever to clean up, or the dozens of eggs that slipped through my fingers. But I remember most of all that when I was twelve years old I was a *bona fide* clerk, standing at the cash register checking out the groceries. I had to stand on a box in order to reach the register, but that didn't matter when I was twelve years old and I was helping my father. He made me feel I was needed. He gave me a sense of dignity and I grew up faster.

That's why I'm so impressed that Jesus lets others help Him. He makes us fellow ministers in His miraculous ministry.

What does this miracle mean for us? It means that John is introducing us to a totally new religion. It is not a religion of rituals, of rules, of regulations, of laws, or of ceremonies, but one that is primarily a belief in a person in whom we can trust and one from whom we receive life. John presents a personal, powerful Lord who turns water to wine, embarrassment to celebration, common existence to extraordinary life. He is indeed, as Jesus later says, *"The way, and the truth, and the life"* (John 14:6).

Back in World War II a prisoner was escaping through the jungle in Malaya. He was being led by a native guide who had sympathized with him. The soldier was nervous because he could see no other human life and no pass through the jungle, so he turned to his guide and asked, "Are you sure this is the way?" And the guide replied in faltering English, "There is no way. I am the way." That's finally what we come down to. In the confusion of this life, being

21

bombarded on every side as we are by advertising and by conflicting values, we ask, "What is the way to life?" And the answer comes back, "There is no charted way. One must follow a guide. He alone knows the way."

We follow Him, this powerful, popular, people-loving Helper of humanity and in following we participate in the joy and laughter of a celebration. The laughter of the wedding symbolizes the joy of the Christian life.

In Jerusalem there is a wailing wall, but it's not for Christians. The sound that you hear from Christians is the sound of music and laughter. As Dr. Matthew, the Dean of St. Paul's wrote so aptly, "Men knew where He had been because of the trail of gladness that He left behind Him."

And His disciples believed in Him.

Footnotes

[1] John W. Doberstein (ed. and trans.), *Christ and the Meaning of Life: A Book of Sermons and Meditations* (Grand Rapids: Baker Book House, © 1962), pp. 120, 121.

Chapter 3

An Unnecessary Miracle

(Mark 4:35-41)

To this day Israelis respect the Sea of Galilee. When we were there recently, more than one resident of Galilee spoke to us about the problems of living by, or earning a living from, that sea. It's not really a sea; it's a lake—a small lake at that—about thirteen miles long and seven miles wide. What makes it treacherous is that it sits so deep in the earth. The lake is about six hundred feet below sea level, surrounded by a high or plateau on either side. At the north end the Jordan River runs into the lake, and at the south it runs out. Several miles to the north is Mount Herman, which rises ninety-one hundred feet above sea level. The uneven terrain produces a very turbulent air situation. Quite often the cold winds come down suddenly from Mount Herman and hit the warmer air nestled in the basin above the water, creating sudden and ruthless storms. It is not at all unusual for a beautiful morning to twist unexpectedly into a stormy afternoon.

On this particular day, Jesus has been at the northern edge of the lake talking from a boat to a large crowd about the kingdom of God. Then at the close of a trying and exhausting day, His disciples take Him in the same boat across the water to the eastern shore. While on the brief crossing, the storm suddenly arises and they are in terrible trouble.

But at the height of the storm, with the winds howling and the waves beating against the boat, the disciples are walking in water well above their ankles

23

as the waves lash over the side of the boat. Jesus sleeps. The others see their danger. They know they may drown, while Jesus rests His head on a cushion in the stern of the boat. He is able to sleep in the midst of the storm because He is in touch with eternity and has no reason to fear.

Hebrews 4 speaks of the reward to which believers look forward—the day when we will be with God. That day has actually already come, Hebrews says. We have entered into our rest. The first several times that I read that passage, the word "rest" didn't mean much to me. It has only been in later years that I've begun to appreciate its significance, because I now realize how few people enjoy true rest.

God has promised us eternal rest at the end of life's turbulence, but He also offers rest that we can enjoy now. Christians can place their confidence in God; they have nothing on earth to fear—even a storm at sea.

Ephesians 4:14 paints another picture. There the apostle Paul is exhorting us to grow up into Christ "so that we may no longer be children, tossed to and fro and carried about with every wind of doctrine" like a boat on the Sea of Galilee. But you can find that stability only if you are secured to things eternal. Martin Luther alluded to this security when he asserted, in one of his most quoted statements, that, while he quietly sat and drank his little mug of Wittenburg beer the gospel ran its course. He could relax from his pressing labors for the Lord because he trusted God to continue to accomplish His purposes.

It is good for us to pause now and then and picture Jesus asleep in the stern of the tossing boat. The disciples are frightened; the Master rests.

I have to defend the disciples, though. They know the lake, and they've seen killing storms suddenly arise before. They probably have been in many of them and they recognize the real danger they are in. They have respect for the water that only the seasoned sailor can fully appreciate.

24

I grew up on the coast of the Pacific Ocean and I learned when I was very young that the old-timers who had spent their lives on and around the sea had profound respect for the water. They would not venture into danger if they could possibly help it.

Jesus' disciples, like those old-timers on the Pacific, know the sea and have a right to be afraid. Furthermore, they know Christ. He is their leader. They have given their lives to Him and they had seen Him do some marvelous things. Peter was especially grateful when Jesus healed his mother-in-law.

They have seen Jesus heal a demon-possessed man, a leper, a paralytic, a man with a withered hand. They have heard His extraordinary teachings. I don't know what they think He should do to save them from the storm now, but they know one thing for sure: He should wake up! They have enough confidence in Him to resent Him.

How quickly belief turns to resentment if the one we believe in lets us down in any way. There's a touch of anger in the disciples' voices as they rebuke Him.

"Jesus, do You not care if we perish?" "Can't You see that we're in danger? How dare You sleep when we need You?" Many of our prayers sound the same, don't they? "God, where were You when I needed You?" "God, where were You when the six million Jews were being exterminated by the Nazis? Where were You in the agonizing days in Vietnam? Where are You when thousands are hungry and crying? Where are You, God?"

Our prayers are usually more personal. "God, I'm in trouble. I can't seem to get through to You. Nothing is happening for me in my terrible situation. God, where are You?" Our belief very quickly turns to resentment. Many and many are the people who have told me that they no longer go to church, or they no longer pray, or they no longer have anything to do with God, because when they needed Him He wasn't there. They resent Him.

Martin Buber, a Jewish theologian, speaking of the horror of concentration camps writes:

> How is a life with God still possible in a time when there is an Auschwitz?" The estrangement has become too cruel, the hiddenness too deep. One can still "believe" in the God who allowed those things to happen, but can one still speak to Him? Can one still hear His word? Can one still . . . enter at all into a dialogic relationship with Him? . . . Dare we recommend to . . . the Job of the gas chambers:
> "Call to Him, for He is kind, for His mercy endureth forever"?[1]

It's a fair question, isn't it? Buber answers that one must never let go of his origin. God *is*, even if He seems to be hiding. "During the day one does not see any stars," but that doesn't mean they're not there.

It is impressive that, even in their panic, when the disciples express their resentfulness, their very words indicate that they believe in Christ. We may cry out against the Lord because He is sleeping, but we still believe in Him enough to call to Him. We are expressing a faith that we may be surprised to discover we have.

Jesus does awake. He first rebukes nature and then He rebukes the disciples. To the wind and the sea, He says, "Peace, be still." To them He says, "Where is your faith?"

Leslie Weatherhead, a prominent British preacher of a generation ago, thinks that Mark made a mistake in his notes here. He says Jesus probably did not stand on the side of the boat and speak to the wind and the sea. Instead, he thinks that Jesus said "Peace, be still" to His disciples, and that only much later was it written down that He said these words to the elements. Weatherhead is worried that naive believers will pervert Christianity into a miraculous instrument to defend themselves and their beloved ones against this world's dangers. He does not want it to be made a thing of magic with God acting as a supernatural magician to whom we turn when we need the winds and the waves calmed. He insists that Christ is not a magician and that religion is not magic. So he changes the story just a little, to make his point.[2]

He's somewhat like the ten-year-old boy who retold his Sunday-school lesson for his mother. The story was about Moses. Moses was dropped behind the enemy lines to rescue the Israelites from the Egyptians, he told her. When they came to the Red Sea, Moses called for engineers to build a pontoon bridge, and after they had all crossed that bridge he looked back and saw Egyptian tanks coming. So he radioed to headquarters with his walkie-talkie and had them send bombers out to blow up the bridge and save the Israelites. His mother said, "Bobby, is that really the way that the teacher told the story?" "Well, not exactly," he said. "But if I told it her way you'd never believe it."

We may be tempted to rewrite Mark 4:35-41 for the same reason, but it's not necessary. I don't have any trouble believing that Jesus spoke to the wind and the sea. Certainly Mark believed He had that power. But don't you also think He spoke to the wind and the sea so that His disciples would overhear Him? The problem was not with the wind and the sea, but with them. *"Why are you afraid? Have you no faith?"*

I have defended their fear of the sea. I would have been afraid, too. But Jesus wants more from them—and us. He wants trust. "If you have faith, you, too, can rest in the midst of a storm." Faith leads to courage, just as love leads to service.

There is an old fable about the little boy who saw a witch turn herself into a cat. The cat began to run after the frightened little boy, who ran away as fast as he could. But when he turned around the cat had grown and become the size of a calf and he was gaining on the boy. When he looked around again the cat had grown even more and was now the size of a house. The little boy ran with all the energy that he had. Finally he couldn't run anymore. There was nothing else to do but to turn and face the danger. So he turned toward the cat. Then the cat retreated, and the farther it ran with the little boy pursuing it the smaller it became until finally it was small enough to scamper back into the witch's house. It's a truthful old fable. Courage *can* chase away the object of one's fear. We need the courage of faith.

We want miracles because we're afraid, but Jesus is more impressed with faith that doesn't require miracles, that faces storms with confidence. Which is better, after all, faith that begs God to interrupt the laws of the universe in order to take care of a few of us who believe in Him, or a faith that believes that no matter what is happening God has us in His embrace and will not let us go? Shouldn't we pray, then, to have courageous faith?

Some very fine Christians have been abused by other believers who have rebuked them in severe illness or a deep personal need, "If you had any faith you'd pray and God would perform a miracle for you." Have you ever heard that? It's unkind, and it's not true to the Bible. For real faith—and we're going to see this repeatedly as we look at the miracles—doesn't ask for the miracles. Real faith yields itself in confidence to the providence of God and then has the courage to accept what God decrees.

The congregation I serve has made me conscious of this bold faith. As my eye surveys the listeners while I preach, I see many people who have suffered deeply, some from bereavement, others from terrible lingering or worsening illness and still others from financial reverses or those awful heartaches that children inflict upon their parents. No miracles have been performed for them. We prayed, they prayed. Some wonderful things happened, but no miracles. But they are still coming to worship the God who provided no miracle, because they've learned that there is something better than a miracle. That something is deep, abiding, encouraging confidence that they are in the hand of God.

What I have just said of the congregation has been true in our family. A few years ago we went through our darkest night. There were no miracles then, either, but we discovered what we hadn't even known about ourselves before: That in the midst of an awful crisis, we could still sleep with the full belief that when one is in touch with eternity, he need not panic. We rested in the storm.

The disciples' question to one another is "What kind of a man is this?" They haven't yet got Jesus' message. He is talking about their faith; they ignore His questions to talk about His character. But sometime they will have to answer Him. They won't for a long time, though. As we follow their career through the Gospels we discover that they don't achieve real courage. Time and again they fail. They're afraid. They are afraid of the religious leaders who try to kill Jesus. They will be afraid of His captors, afraid to be identified with Him. They will be afraid at times to trust His judgment. They will live with fear until after His resurrection.

That's why Jesus must try to turn their attention away from the miracle to the meaning of faith. He wants to help them to grow beyond fear into confidence so that they can sleep in the storms to come. One day they will find rest in Him.

Among my favorite hymns is this one:

When peace, like a river, attendeth my way,
  When sorrows like sea billows roll,
Whatever my lot, Thou hast taught me to say,
  It is well, it is well with my soul.
If it is, then you can sleep.

Footnotes

[1]*At the Turning: Three Addresses on Judaism* (New York: Farrar, Straus and Young, 1952), p. 61.

[2]*When the Lamp Flickers* (Nashville: Abingdon-Cokesbury Press, © 1948, by Pierce & Smith), p. 65.

Chapter 4

A Miracle—
For a While

(Matthew 14:22-36; Mark 6:47-51; John 6:16-21)

We return to stormy Galilee. Once again Jesus relieves His disciples' distress as they battle fierce waves on the wind-battered lake. We called Jesus' calming of the angry sea an unnecessary miracle, for His primary concern was not with the terrifying storm, but with His followers' lack of courageous faith. He calmed the storm in order to gain a hearing for His rebuke, "Why are you afraid? Have you no faith?" The real threat to them was not in the winds and waves, but in their fear. Miracles were not difficult for the Master of tempests, but leading His disciples to courage was an arduous, slow process. It still is. For this reason, He bolsters our unsteady faith by coming to us as we face our crises.

We certainly need Him, so even as He challenges us to be brave in the storm He stands by as our abiding companion while the waves beat against us. In the tempests of Galilee we feel the recurring blows we suffer in life. The disciples' distress is ours, too. It was especially perplexing for them because it was Jesus who ordered them to cross the lake at that treacherous hour without Him, so that He could retreat into the hills to pray. The Lord's order had sent them into grave danger. They must have grumbled about this injustice, just as we complain when God seems apathetic about the injuries inflicted on us in the course of our service for Him.

There is something more distressful than the Lord's absence in our time of need, however, and that

31

is His unexpected presence. When the disciples saw Jesus walking on the sea they were terrified. They didn't recognize Him; they had never dreamed that He might not be subject to the usual limitations of human existence. Although they had witnessed His miraculous power over illness and even over the wind and sea, they could not conceive that the power that raised the paralytic could suspend Jesus on the water.

Christ frequently shatters our preconceptions of Him like this. He will not remain comfortably in our categories. He resists our explanations, breaks out of our definitions of Him, and when He catches us off guard, we become afraid. Just when we think we have Him under our control, He exercises His freedom—more than that, He asserts His lordship and forces us to acknowledge that He is not altogether of this world.

That is why He so quickly speaks to assuage their fears. *"Take heart, it is I; have no fear"* (Matthew 14:27). He is not a ghost. While not shackled by human limitations, He is nonetheless still their friend Jesus, with whom they have eaten and drunk and in whose company they have found comfort. He has come to them because of their distress. He is now doing for them what He came into the world to do for all who believe in Him: He has come to rescue them (see John 3:16).

"It is I." These simple words *(ego eimi)* mean more than is immediately apparent. With these words God revealed himself to Moses (Exodus 3:14) and with them Jesus repeatedly expresses His divine nature. (See John 6:35: *"I am the bread of life"*; John 8:12 and 9:5: *"I am the light of the world"*; John 8:58: *"Before Abraham was, I am"*; John 10:9: *"I am the door"*; John 10:11: *"I am the good shepherd"*; John 11:25: *"I am the resurrection and the life"*; and John 15:1: *"I am the true vine."*) Jesus has just come from communion with God in prayer. There, apart from the press of the crowds, He was reminded of His

32

other-worldly origin and power. When He identifies himself for His disciples, His words carry more than their immediate sense: "I am Jesus your friend but, as you can see by my unexpected appearance on the water, I am more than you yet know of me. 'I am' unlike any other. I am among you, but not wholly one of you. Yet what you see me doing is within your grasp."

Peter, so often impulsive yet so often right in his impulses, seems intuitively to grasp the significance of Jesus' startling appearance. *"Lord, if it is you, bid me come to you on the water."* Peter knows of Jesus' superhuman powers intimately. It took an extraordinary personality to lure Peter away from his fishing; it was an extraordinary human being who could so quickly restore his mother-in-law to health. And Peter has just watched in amazement as Jesus provided lunch for a crowd of more than five thousand. If the ghost is really Jesus, then it will be nothing for Him to enable Peter to join Him on the water.

So Peter asks for an invitation. Here, as on so many other occasions, Peter shows the bold spontaneity which makes him such an able—if at times wrong-headed—leader. No other disciple speaks up. They cannot be so brash. They undoubtedly are shocked and critical of Peter, castigating him for so frequently leaping into things before looking. But, as someone has said, it is better not to look before leaping than, as most men do, to look so long that they never leap.

Peter is still the butt of many jokes for his folly in trying to walk on water. What men's laughter often ignores, however, is this sobering truth: He did in fact walk on water. That's the miracle. It's a miracle of faith that demonstrates the courage faith engenders. Peter does the impossible. Jesus bids him *"Come,"* and he obeys, just as he obediently left his fishnets months before to follow this magnetic, demanding Lord. It must have seemed impossible then to turn his back on his livelihood and devote himself exclusively

33

to Jesus, but he did it. To everyone in the boat, Peter included, the impossibility of walking on water is undisputed. But he does it. A very successful American leader once told Robert Schuller, "I have never done anything in my life that did not seem impossible when I was in the beginning stage." I know what he's talking about. Everything worthwhile I have ever tried seemed overwhelming if not impossible in the beginning. Had I looked only at the obstacles, they would have paralyzed me. One has to respond instead to the "Come."

That is the difference between Peter and the others in the boat. One dared to leave the boat and venture into the impossibility. He took the leap of faith. In Browning's poem, "Paracelsus," the hero asks his friend Festus if there are not really two moments in a pearl diver's life:

One—when, a beggar, he prepares to plunge?
One—when, a prince, he rises with his pearl?
Festus, I plunge!

There are no pearls for those who remain in the boat, or only prepare to dive for the treasure. It requires courage to test the impossible and prove it possible.

Peter must be named among the courageous. He dares to obey his Lord's call.

His success does not last, however. He has made a magnificent start toward his goal. What an exhilarating moment it is for him to venture beyond the borders of human experience, if even just for an instant to conquer both his fear and the forces of nature. But then he invites defeat: he turns his eyes from his goal to his difficulty. He looks at the wind. His courage deserts him and he feels himself slipping into the threatening waters. His heroic effort has collapsed. Doubt defeats faith.

How quickly faith gives way to fear. You probably are familiar with this famous illustration: Suppose someone were to place on the ground a plank thirty feet long by one foot wide. You would have no trouble walking from one end of the plank to the other

34

without stepping off. But suppose the plank were elevated the height of a high building, say a church steeple. Could you then make the same walk without falling off? Would you even be willing to try?

Why not? The plank is the same length and width. If you could traverse it easily on the ground, should you not be able to do so at the elevated level? The problem, obviously, is not with the plank, but with your fears. Because you imagine it is easy to walk the plank on the ground, you easily do it. Because you imagine all the difficulties involved in crossing the plank at a high elevation, your doubts impede and finally defeat you. Like Peter, you will be "seeing the wind."

I have read several articles recently in which prominent physicians decry the growing reliance of Americans upon the so-called annual physical check-up. To look for something wrong is to find it. It's no secret that if you go to a doctor often enough and he looks hard enough he's going to find something wrong with you. If you are a typical person, you'll become so convinced of your newly discovered weakness you'll never be strong again.

It's a fact that most of the world's really successful men and women have the same afflictions as those who remain in their boats of mediocrity. Instead of giving way to their disabilities, however, they act like Murrow's British in the "ignorance of their weakness."

Edward R. Murrow, attempting to account for Britain's incredible courage before overwhelming odds in the bleak early days of World War II, found part of the explanation in what he called the English "ignorance of their own weakness."[1] I like that phrase, if only because most of us have an excessive knowledge of our weakness. We appraise ourselves to be weaker than we are, thereby guaranteeing the debility we fear. Had Peter had time to think about it, he would have known he couldn't walk on water; but he didn't analyze his situation in the beginning, he

35

just walked. It was later that the reality of his situation dawned on him. "I can't do this," he told himself. Then he couldn't.

Peter leaps ahead of the others and he fails—yet not entirely. Something of his success lingers. Of the others remaining in the boat the Gospel tells us nothing. It concentrates on the man who dares a miracle and almost completes it. He fails, yes, but his is a magnificent failure. It is a failure far more glorious than any success the boat riders could boast of. Millions of unknown men and women never fail simply because they never try. Peter outlives them all. He has tried!

His resources run out, however, and he has to call for help. "Lord, save me." Here is another indication of Peter's faith in Christ. He cannot save himself but he can trust his Lord to rescue him. Immediately Jesus reaches out and Peter is safe.

Sam Stone tells of a black student in Fisk University who was on board a steamer that caught fire. The student made his wife and himself safe by fastening life preservers on, but in the ensuing panic someone tore his wife's preserver from her, leaving her helpless in the water. She clung to her husband with her hands on his shoulders, trying to remain afloat, but she was soon exhausted and could not hold on any longer.

"Try a little bit more," he pleaded, then added, "Let's sing 'Rock of Ages.'"

So they did. Other swimmers nearby heard them and joined in with them. "Rock of Ages, cleft for me, Let me hide myself in Thee" the nearly exhausted swimmers sang above the waves. Their strength returned and sustained them until the lifeboat rescued them. They could also have sung with Washington Gladden:

> In the bitter waves of woe,
> Beaten and tossed about
> By the sullen winds that blow
> O'er the desolate shores of doubt,

When the anchors that faith had cast
        Are dragging in the gale,
I am quietly holding fast
        To the things that cannot fail.

Like Peter, they were clasped by the Master's unfailing hand and were saved.[2]

Peter must have been somewhat shocked when Jesus, instead of congratulating him on his bravery, scolded him for his doubt. *"O man of little faith, why did you doubt"* Had Peter not just done far more than anyone, including himself, had ever thought possible? That may be so, but Jesus insisted that he could have done more had his original faith not wavered. *"Nothing will be impossible to you"* (Matthew 17:21) is a recurring theme in Jesus' teaching, words that too many of us receive with appreciation but without belief.

Not only does Jesus not commend Peter here; we discover to our surprise that Jesus never complimented His disciples on their great faith. Once a Canaanite woman begged Jesus to deliver her daughter from demon possession; when He resisted, saying He was *"sent only to the lost sheep of the house of Israel,"* she continued to beg until Jesus said to her, *"O woman, great is your faith!"* (Matthew 15:21-28). On another occasion Jesus said of a centurion who besought him to cure his paralyzed servant, *"Truly, I say to you, not even in Israel have I found such faith"* (Matthew 8:5-13). But of His own disciples' faith he said nothing. What distinguished the centurion and the Syrophonecian woman from them? Just this: they both came to Jesus with outstretched hands, asking the impossible and believing implicitly in Jesus' ability to do it. The disciples believed in large measure, quite obviously so, but not completely, not without reservation. They still looked too much to the wind.

Faith is aware of the wind but looks instead on the Lord. Tempests threaten us less when we hold our gaze steadfast on His calming face. We understand Him to be *"the image of the invisible God"* (Colos-

37

sians 1:15); we trust Him to come to us in the storms of our lives as He came to the disciples and brought peace. The Almighty God might seem too distant to help us, but the Christ who rescues His disciples is very like a friend indeed.

This incident on Galilee was sung by a psalmist long before it happened to the disciples. Listen to Psalm 107:23-31:

"Some went down to the sea in ships,
   doing business on the great waters;
they saw the deeds of the Lord,
   his wondrous works in the deep.
For he commanded, and raised the stormy wind,
   which lifted up the waves of the sea.
They mounted up to heaven,
   they went down to the depths;
Their courage melted away in their evil plight;
   they reeled and staggered like drunken men,
   and were at their wits' end.
Then they cried to the Lord in their trouble,
   and he delivered them from their distress;
He made the storm be still,
   and the waves of the sea were hushed.
Then they were glad because they had quiet,
   and he brought them to their desired haven.
Let them thank the Lord for his steadfast love,
   for his wonderful works to the sons of men!"

What Jesus did for His disciples God has always done for His people. Is it any wonder, then, that the disciples worshiped Him, saying, "Truly you are the Son of God"? We worship for the same reason.

Footnotes

   [1]*This I Believe.* (New York: Simon & Schuster, © 1952), p. 11.
   [2]Sam Stone, *Grounded Faith for Growing Christians.* (Cincinnati: Standard Publishing, © 1975) pp. 56, 57.

Chapter 5

A Glimpse
of Eternity

(Matthew 17:1-9; Mark 9:2-8; Luke 9:28-36)

You probably won't recognize the name of Horace Walpole. There isn't really any reason you should, for he lived in eighteenth-century England and has had almost no influence on our century—almost none, that is, except to one man whose life he has shaped and dominated.

The man's name is Wilmarth S. Lewis. In 1933 he began his life's work of editing Walpole's correspondence. By 1973, forty years after he had begun, Lewis at seventy-seven had completed thirty-seven three-inch-thick volumes of Walpole's letters and had thirteen to go. The finished set would have seven thousand pieces of correspondence.

Not many persons who have ever lived are important enough to elicit such devotion. Walpole was a prominent writer in his time, composing political diaries and fiction, editing art books and writing letters that offer valuable information about the life and customs of his England. We can appreciate the contribution that Lewis' singleminded devotion to the project has made to the scholarship of the period. Nonetheless, many of us would question why any person should give his whole life to the task of preserving someone else's mail.

Lewis' defense is quite straightforward. He had started collecting things as a youngster, he admitted, including such delights as houseflies, seashells, stamps, coins, butterflies, and books. By 1923 he had acquired a thousand books in English literature, but then found he was not really interested in them. "Yet I knew," he concluded, "if I could get interested in one person, I could have a direction for life." The person he selected was Walpole.[1]

Universities and colleges are populated by scholars who have adopted Lewis' philosophy. They have become experts in Shakespeare or Plato or Beethoven or Rembrandt. I was tempted to follow their example myself, flirting for a while with the idea of becoming an expert in Robert Browning. My interest didn't last long, however. I discovered that, even though he is among the most interesting poets of the English language, his voice isn't strong enough to hold my attention for a lifetime. I need more.

Years ago a small band of men obeyed a summons to follow a young itinerant Preacher in the rugged countryside of Galilee. Impressed by His extraordinary personality and His amazing gifts of healing and teaching, they seem almost impulsively to have left their homes and businesses to devote themselves to His crusade. When He spoke they caught His every syllable; no man had ever spoken to them like this Man. To them it seemed His words rang with the authority of eternity. They believed they had chosen to follow the one person who could give direction for their lives.

God confirmed their choice. High on a mountain they beheld a sight so spectacular they dared tell no one about it until long after, until an even greater miracle—a resurrection—had occurred. They beheld their Master glowing with a radiance unparalleled, conversing comfortably with two of the greatest heroes of all time. They watched in hushed awe as a brilliant cloud passed over them and a voice from eternity spoke to them. Then they knew that the one they were following was himself a glimpse of God, His voice the voice of eternity, and His words the truth to build a life on.

"Listen to him," God said. Listen to Him even above your greatest religious leaders.

To the Jews Moses had no peer. He was their ancestors' redeemer. They called him "savior," for he had led his people from slavery in Egypt to freedom in the promised land. He was their great lawgiver. He had himself ascended high into the mountain and later descended with the words of God. Yet now the voice of God was saying, "Listen to Jesus."

The Jews honored Elijah above all other prophets. This great speaker for God had boldly defied the seven hundred priests of Baal and all the might of the infamous Jezebel. As the centuries passed following those mighty feats, his fame increased until he surpassed the other prophets in importance. He would be, the Jew believed, the messenger divinely appointed to announce the coming of the promised One of God, the Messiah. Yet the voice of God was saying, "Listen to Jesus."

Had Peter, James, and John been contemporary Americans instead of first-century Jews, I wonder whom they would have seen there beside Jesus. It is an indication of our secular age that I cannot think of any religious leader we would immediately recognize. Some religious persons might see the Pope or Sun Myung Moon, or Mahara Ji, or Martin Luther, John Calvin, or Alexander Campbell. Would we expect to see Mary Baker Eddy, Kathryn Kuhlman, Oral Roberts, or Billy Graham? Most Americans would not have recognized any one of these persons.

Since religious leaders would scarcely be recognized, is it possible that we might not even recognize the voice of God? Has our age become so noisy that we tuned God out long ago? I have a friend who cannot sleep without first turning on the television or radio. He learned the trick a few years ago. By turning the volume up so the sound is perceptible but the words are not distinguishable, the noise of the TV or radio cancels out the other noises from the street and house. Then he can sleep.

I have adoped the same plan. There are times when our home is very noisy. The kids' radio is playing in a bedroom, the TV is on in the family room. Some-one is playing the piano while another is on either the clarinet or the violin. When they are all going at the same time—except for Lane's trombone—I can sleep. All the noises cancel each other out.

There is danger in all the noise of our century, however. We may be lulled permanently to sleep. Religious leaders after a while sound alike; they all want our devotion, our time, our money. They all promise eternal bliss if we follow them, eternal dam-nation if we don't. To whom should we listen? All our politicians pledge to work for our welfare. If we elect them we shall enter into a period of prosperity and peace. So we elect them, but their visions of glory turn to horror. Who is right? Where is the truth? To whom should we give ourselves?

We need a voice from eternity as much as the disciples did. God's word to them is His word to us: When you listen to my Son you are hearing the truth; when you obey Him you are doing the highest of which you are capable; when you are in Him you enter eternity. Listen to *Him* instead of other religious leaders.

Listen to Him in spite of His suffering.

Just a few days before this mountaintop moment, Jesus had begun preparing His disciples for the in-evitable. The growing hostilities of the scribes and Pharisees could lead to only one resolution: Jesus must be killed. *"God forbid, Lord! This shall never happen to you,"* Peter protested. Only recently he had begun to understand that Jesus was not just an-other human being but God's promised Messiah, the Christ. If that were true, and Peter fervently believed it to be, then his Master would be invincible, for who could raise a hand against God's elect?

Peter was not alone in his refusal to accept Jesus' predictions. James and John had visions of grandeur, also. They and their mother looked forward to the day when Jesus would reign as Lord of the earth, and they would be His chief lieutenants.

42

We understand them. We want to win. We don't want to be on the losing captain's team. I still remember trying to play football or baseball as a kid, out in the vacant lot or at school. I hated it when the two captains would choose up the sides. They always picked the best first, leaving the nonathletes like me until the very end. Then I would predictably be selected to play for the losing side.

Nobody likes to lose, but in the weeks ahead, Jesus will look very much like a loser. A voice from Heaven is needed to reassure the disciples in the dark days to come that, despite all appearances, God has not abandoned His Son. The shining face and clothing, like Moses' as he descended the mountain with the tables of Commandments in his hands (Exodus 34:29) and the brilliant cloud of glory, are easily recognized by the disciples as signs of God's presence. (See Exodus 34:29; 13:21, 22; 16:6, 7; 19:9, etc.) Surely God is speaking. This *is* His Son. He will not abandon Him—and neither should you disciples desert Him.

What Peter does not yet understand (Matthew 16:24-28) is that the triumphant Messiah can triumph only through sacrifice. His ministry can be authenticated only by His death, His lordship only by the resurrection. There is no escape. Jesus must suffer, but especially in His suffering His followers must listen to Him, for suffering will lead to God's victory.

Fox's *Book of Martyrs* records Christianity's victory over Rome's gladiatorial contests. These legal butcheries had become the chief spectator sport of Rome, annually slaughtering hundreds of the contestants who dueled to their deaths before roaring crowds. To Christians, who accounted every human being as of infinite worth, the existence of the contests was repugnant, but they were helpless to stop them. Helpless, that is, until one man from the wilds of Asia, Telemachus by name, came to Rome to preach against this brutal form of murder. In the midst of one of the contests his rudely clad figure appeared

43

in the audience, then boldly leaped into the arena and advanced toward the gladiators, laying a hand on them and scolding them for participating in the bloodshed. Then Telemachus turned, facing the angry thousands and speaking with a voice like one from Heaven.

"This is no place for preaching!" the spectators roared back. "The old customs of Rome must be observed! On, gladiators!" But the courageous man stood between the gladiators, preventing their contest, until, as the crowd rained stones down upon him, they stabbed him to death. Then, in shock, the people realized what they had done and they left, emptying the coliseum. That was the effective end of the gladiatorial contests.

The evil had to be stopped. Only a human sacrifice could do it. *This is my beloved Son, . . . listen to him,* therefore, in spite of His coming suffering.

"Listen to Him," even when you are no longer on the mountaintop.

It will be hard for the disciples to remember the voice of God when facing the same torture that Jesus suffered. "No, I don't even know who He is" Peter will shout to his accusers (Matthew 26). When they encounter the world's hatred which Christ foretells for them (John 15:18 ff), it will not be easy to resist the urge to desert Him. "Listen to Him" in the battles below as you are listening now in the isolated splendor of this mountaintop.

Among Raphael's very greatest paintings is his rendition of "The Transfiguration" which is still on display in the Vatican in Rome. At the top and center of the picture is Christ, with Moses and Elijah slightly below and beside Him. Just beneath, awed by the magnificent spectacle above them, are Peter, James, and John. At the foot of the mountain are the other disciples, trying to cure a demon-possessed boy. But the disciples are helpless. They cannot cure him. Some of the disciples have taken their eyes from their problem and are pointing upward to the transfigured

Christ, as if to say, "There is the source of healing power." The painting is a graphic reminder that Christ did not come to earth to dazzle His disciples with His other worldly glory. His real mission is below, with the demented boy. And though His three closest disciples have been favored with this glimpse of eternity, they must follow Him down the mountainside and immerse themselves in the world's pain. The descent is essential.

Archibald Rutledge somewhere tells of the widow of a black preacher who was constantly doing what she could to lighten the burdens of the poor, orphaned, and illegitimate children in her community. He was so touched with her charity that he built her a little house in his own backyard. He even furnished it for her and invited her to make it hers. This she gladly did, but she horrified Rutledge when she invited in the most disreputable black woman in the country. With amazement and exasperation he asked her how she could invite that creature into her new home. Her answer was quiet but firm: "Jesus would." She had grasped the central fact of the gospel. Jesus did not come to be transfigured on a mountain, but to serve in the valleys. His followers will do likewise.

But it is much easier to stay on the mountain, where the pure breezes blow and the stench and sounds of the sick and poor are far beneath. If only Christ would have allowed Peter and James and John to stay up there with Him forever.

But He didn't.

"Listen to Him," because He *alone* is God's Son, His beloved. Moses and Elijah have been eclipsed, and with them all other claimants for our worship have been overshadowed. There is only one, as Peter was later to acknowledge when Jesus, noting that many of His followers were deserting, asked him whether he would also go away. *"Lord, to whom shall we go? You have the words of eternal life; and we have believed, and have come to know, that you are the Holy One of God"* (John 6:68, 69).

He alone is worthy of our adoration. Peter cannot build three small booths; only Christ deserves our reverence, and He cannot be confined to a shrine. He is Lord, and those who worship Him will bring all they are and have into subjection to Him.

Strange, isn't it, that others often understand the real meaning of faith which sometimes escapes a Christian's comprehension? In September, 1977, Gordon Liddy, former counsel to President Richard Nixon's reelection committee, was released from federal prison in Danbury, Connecticut. He had been behind bars for more than fifty-two months, his punishment for his role in the Nixon administration's Watergate scandal. When he was asked to explain the part he played in the infamous plot, he answered, "When the prince approaches his lieutenant, the proper response of the lieutenant is *'Fiat voluntas tua'* " (Thy will be done). The lieutenant hears only one voice, the voice of his prince.

Gordon Liddy was wrong because his prince was wrong, but he understood the meaning of the words, "Listen to him."

The first Commandment which Moses had delivered to the people was this: *"You shall have no other gods before me."* That Commandment has never been rescinded. To worship any other than God himself is idolatry. Elijah, then, is unworthy of our allegiance. Even Moses himself, the great lawgiver, cannot claim our loyalty. Only one remains: "This is my beloved Son. Listen to Him."

Footnotes

[1] *Time*, October 29, 1973, p. 100.

Chapter 6

Seeing Is Believing
(John 9)

The best freedoms of all we don't celebrate. They aren't guaranteed by our Constitution, they weren't secured by the War of Independence. We take them for granted and even abuse them until we meet someone like the remarkable man in John 9 who has lived his life deprived of one of them. The best freedoms are those granted by the senses—sight, hearing, taste, feeling, and smell. To be without them is a type of captivity. One who cannot see is not less human, of course, but his mobility is restricted and his life is decidedly more complicated.

In one of the New Testament's most remarkable incidents, Jesus meets a man denied his freedom of sight from birth, and He sets him free. The miracle is briefly related, but the debate it triggers between Jesus' opponents and the healed man is carefully detailed. The narrative turns on several penetrating questions. We shall concentrate on those questions.

Whose fault is it that this man is blind? Jesus' disciples probably raise the question casually, not anticipating that He will do anything for the man. The issue arises naturally because it is one that is never far from their consciousness. We are equally troubled about the causes of physical maladies, but we would not ask in the same words. We would seek, instead, an organic cause, dismissing as an antiquated notion their assumption that physical illness is related to moral behavior.

47

They have no doubt, however, that sin is involved, for according to Rabbi Ammi, "There is no death without sin, and there is no suffering without iniquity." Job's friend Eliphaz the Temanite shared the same conviction:

"Think now, who that was innocent ever perished?
Or where were the upright cut off?
As I have seen, those who plow iniquity
and sow trouble reap the same" (Job 4:7, 8).

The disciples have no hesitancy, then, in attributing the man's blindness to sin. But his situation is complicated by the fact that he was born with the disability. Had the condition come upon him later, he could have been charged with sin. Since he was born with the affliction, however, is it fair to blame him? Some Jewish thinkers believed it is, teaching that one could somehow commit sin even in his mother's womb. To others, such reasoning was foolish.

If not the man, then, was it his parent's fault? The commentary on the second Commandment (Exodus 20:4 ff) could be used to condemn them: "I the Lord your God am a jealous God, visiting the iniquity of the fathers upon the children to the third and the fourth generation of those who hate me." Today scientists and physicians warn us that certain habits (smoking tobacco, drinking alcohol, using drugs) can have serious physical consequences on our descendants. Moralists have long pointed out that immoral behavior in one generation can do permanent damage to children and grandchildren. "He is a wise man who chooses a good grandfather," Oliver Wendell Holmes said. So the disciples' question makes sense.

It is a little surprising that they did not ask one more. **"Is it God's fault?"** must have been in their hearts if not on their lips, for the passage in Exodus leaves little doubt that it is God who visits the iniquity upon the descendants, and the passage from Job continues: "By the breath of God they perish, and by the blast of his anger they are consumed" (Job 4:9).

Listen to Exodus 4:11: *"Then the Lord said to [Moses], 'Who has made man's mouth? Who makes him dumb, or deaf, or seeing, or blind? Is it not I, the Lord?'"*

So strong was the conviction of the ancient Israelites that God was involved in their daily lives, they could not conceive that He had nothing to do with their illnesses. They knew themselves to be sinners, disappointing their holy God. He had not only the right but even the parental responsibility to punish their wickedness.

Who has made the man blind—himself, his parents, or God? Disturbingly enough, Jesus does not answer directly. Throughout His ministry He steadfastly refuses to answer complex theological questions with simple answers. Now is not the moment for debate, His silence suggests; here is a human being to heal. Instead of defending or explaining, He says, "This is my opportunity to demonstrate the work of God. *As long as I am in the world, I am the light of the world.* My job is to give sight to the physically blind as well as the spiritually blinded."

We cannot observe Jesus' healing of this beggar (for what else could a blind man do in the first century?) without pausing over the fourth verse: *"We must work the works of him who sent me, while it is day."* Jesus is the light of the world (verse 5), but His *we* includes those He has commissioned to carry on His work. To them He has said, *"You are the light of the world"* (Matthew 5:14). His healing ministry continues through His disciples. The question has now changed. No longer do we ask, "Whose fault is it that this man is blind?" We must instead find out how we Christians can participate with Him in bringing light to eyes that have not seen. For, as Frank Laubauch has said, when Christ who is the way enters into us, "we become part of the Way. God's highway runs straight through us." We are partners with Christ in light-bearing. The real thrill for Christians is not in living the so-called good life, but, as Paul Scherer has

exclaimed, "The fundamental joy of it is in standing with God against some darkness or some void and watching the light come,"[1] as it comes into the eyes of this blind beggar.

"Then how were your eyes opened?" Not everyone rejoices when light comes. First the question must be settled: how could this happen? When a man has not seen for all of his life, how could his useless eyes begin to function so suddenly?

The man cannot answer. He can only tell them who, not how. *"The man called Jesus made clay and anointed my eyes and said to me, 'Go to Siloam and wash'; so I went and washed and received my sight."* I only did what I was told. That's all I know.

A little more is implied than this. He mentions the clay made from the dust and spittle. In Jesus' day there was a widespread belief in the healing power of human saliva. Although Jesus seldom made use of any "props" in His miracles, He does take advantage here of that common belief and employs the methods of His time. The Scripture makes very little of these elements, however. Something far more important is emphasized.

That something is the man's obedience. Jesus tells him to go and wash and he obeys. Without the obedience there would be no healing. The purpose for the clay is to test the man's willingness to do the Lord's bidding.

One of the principal themes of the Bible is *obedience*. Adam and Eve fell through disobedience. Abraham became the friend of God because, as God said, *"You have obeyed my voice"* (Genesis 22:18). His promises to Israel had one condition: *"If you will obey my voice and keep my covenant"* (Exodus 19:5). King Saul was reminded that *"to obey is better than sacrifice"* (1 Samuel 15:22). Peter and John deserve our admiration because they could say to hostile officials, *"We must obey God rather than men"* (Acts 5:29). The promise of God's Spirit is conditional: *". . . the Holy Spirit whom God has given to*

51

those who obey Him" (Acts 5:32). There is nothing casual about the injunction to obey the voice of the Lord; it is a central Biblical theme.

It is probably this passage's emphasis upon obedience, more than the mention of the pool of Siloam, which made it a favorite baptismal text among early Christians. It appears seven times in early catacomb art as an illustration for Christian baptism. The text is frequently found in early Christian liturgical books to prepare converts for baptism. The Christians saw a relationship between his healing in the water and the cleansing, renewing experience of baptism. They also recognized that the first stirrings of faith in Christ must be followed by some act of obedience. Peter acknowledged this need when he concluded his Pentecost sermon with the exhortation, "*Repent, **and** be baptized*" (Acts 2:38); new faith in Christ has to be exhibited in a change of life's direction and an *act* demonstrating obedience to the Lord. Obedience is what faith is all about.

The man's eyes are opened through the cooperation of the Lord's power and his own humble obedience.

"Who is he, then?" is the real question, or as the Pharisees phrased it, "*What do you say about him, since he has opened your eyes?*" By this time they are convinced that Jesus is a sinner. Their opposition does not shake the newly-healed man, however. "*He is a prophet.*" He knows very little about Jesus and doesn't pretend to. He believes in God, however, and knows that God endowed the ancient prophets with miraculous power. Since Jesus has powers that he has never known anyone else to have, Jesus must be one of God's specially chosen spokesmen, like Elijah or Amos.

Even when the exasperated Pharisees rebuke him—"*Give God the praise; we know that this man is a sinner,*" they cannot shake his loyalty to his Healer: "*Whether he is a sinner, I do not know; one thing I know, that though I was blind, now I see.*" He

52

refuses to play their game. They fancy themselves to be experts in the law; they love to make pronouncements about God's character and will for people. They can argue the subleties of theological doctrines. All that is beyond the humble man. But what he knows he knows: Christ has given him sight and for that favor he will not betray Him.

We watch the man's faith grow in this encounter. Jesus is first simply a *"man called Jesus"* (v. 11), then a prophet (v. 17), then a man from God (v. 33), and finally the Son of man whom he can worship (vv. 35-38). At the same time the Pharisees, blinded by their doctrinal prejudices, become increasingly bitter. They begin by insisting that Jesus is not from God (v. 16), proceed to question the indisputable evidence that a miracle has occurred (v. 18), then to speak of Jesus as a sinner (v. 24). Finally, even the unlearned beggar realizes that they are ignorant men (v. 30) and Jesus dismisses them as spiritually blind sinners (v. 41). How pathetically blind they look beside the now-seeing former beggar, who looks at—worships—Jesus.

"Would you teach us? The arrogant Pharisees are proud to be certified religious leaders. They refuse to learn from a beggar. They are the experts, not he.

Harry Truman knew some experts and refused to be intimidated by them. This is how he defined them: "I said that an expert was a fella who was afraid to learn anything new, because then he wouldn't be an expert anymore."[2] That is precisely the Pharisee's plight. They cannot admit that Jesus is other than a sinner, or they lose their credibility as experts in religion.

God frequently uses the humble to teach the proud, however. A blind man instructs Pharisees, the son of a carpenter judges them. *"For judgment I came into this world,"* Jesus tells them, *"that those who do not see may see, and that those who see may become blind."* He has elevated the humble and humbled the mighty. E. Stanley Jones recalls a custom among his

Christian friends in India who would volunteer to take the place of an outcast sweeper one day a week in order to give the man a holiday. This scavenging work was not easy for either white or brown Brahmins. To clean a latrine was far, far beneath them. One Brahmin convert hesitated to do the work and Jones asked him when he was going to volunteer. He drew a long breath and slowly replied, "Well, I'm converted, but I am not converted that far."[3]

Yet, said Jesus, "He who would be great among you must be servant of all." Because the Pharisees cannot stoop to learn from the beggar—they are not converted that far—the Lord has to condemn them. He can heal a blind man but can offer little but pity to the proud in spirit. So the Pharisees are replaced as teachers by a humble peasant who has no claim to authority but one, the all-important one of experience. He cannot expound the Scriptures with the learned doctors, but he can testify, *Though I was blind, now I see.*

He has met the Lord. He has been healed by the Lord. He will therefore not betray his Lord.

Footnotes

[1] *Love Is a Spendthrift* (New York: Harper & Brothers, publishers, © 1961), p. 210.

[2] Merle Miller, *Plain Speaking: An Oral Biography of Harry S. Truman* (New York: Berkley Publishing, © 1973, 1974), p. 233.

[3] *Christ's Alternative to Communism* (New York, Cincinnati, Chicago: Abingdon Press, © 1935), p. 292.

The Joy of Being Whole
(Luke 13:10-17)

Jesus does not have to heal the woman. She is in the synagogue, but she is not part of His group. Because it is the Sabbath, nobody expects a healing and nobody asks for it. Why, then, does He call the woman over to Him to set her free? Since He has just been teaching, can the miracle be His way of applying the words of Scripture, of uniting religion and life? He has always insisted, "I must be a doer of the Word and not a teacher only." If this is His purpose, what does this healing teach us as well as those who saw Him touch the woman?

At the least, Jesus' action demonstrates that talking about God often isn't good enough, even in the synagogue. We must *do* the word of God. We are frequently tempted to substitute Bible study for active service for God. We are all familiar with James' injunction, *"Be doers of the word, and not hearers only, deceiving yourselves"* (1:22). Jesus' action here seems to be a variation on the same theme: "Be doers of the word, not talkers only." To His teaching He adds action. *"We must work the works of him who sent me,"* He instructed His disciples on another occasion, *"while it is day"* (John 9:4).

From the beginning Jesus has combined teaching with healing. He inaugurated His ministry in His hometown by opening the Scriptures to Isaiah 61:1, which He applied to himself:

"The Spirit of the Lord is upon me, because he has anointed me to preach good news to the poor. He

55

has sent me to proclaim release to the captives and recovering of sight to the blind, to set at liberty those who are oppressed, to proclaim the acceptable year of the Lord" (Luke 4:18, 19).

God had commissioned Jesus to more than a teaching ministry ("anointed me to preach good news"); it was to be a serving one as well (release the captives, give sight to the blind, free the oppressed). Word must be applied in deed.

Jesus and His disciples seek to enact the gospel, then, wherever they are—even in the synagogue. There is a woman who has suffered eighteen years from spinal fusion. Jesus picks her out, as He earlier spotted a man with a withered hand (Mark 3), taking the initiative to heal them where they least expect it. Others have attended the synagogue with these crippled persons for years without really paying any attention to them. They have been just faces in the crowd, no more. To Jesus, however, they are afflicted human beings needing the touch of love. He puts His talk into action.

In doing do, Jesus teaches that **persons are more important than systems.**

The ruler of the synagogue, the leader of the council of ten Jewish men who control the teaching and activities there, is incensed at Jesus' behavior. He doesn't speak directly to Him, lacking the courage to deal with Him personally, but scolds the crowd for being party to this breach of Sabbath decorum. He refuses to join in the gaiety surrounding the newly healed woman. His beloved system has been violated and he will not allow it to be disturbed again.

The ruler is undoubtedly not a bad man. He enjoys the respect of his fellow Jews as a learned and spiritual man. He loves God, but he has lost his sense of values. It is disturbingly easy to disregard human needs in the name of religious duty.

He is not a bad man, as I said, but he is a hypocrite. That's Jesus word for him, and others like him, who will tolerate human suffering in the name of religious tradition. *Hypocrite* means play actor. "You're only playing at religion." Jesus accuses him, "or you would know that talking about the love of God isn't good enough. You must apply it to those who most need it, wherever and whenever you find them, like here and now with this woman. You would untie your ox or ass from the manger, wouldn't you? Is it then so wrong to untie this woman from the bonds that have crippled her for these eighteen years?"

Jesus has faithfully observed the Sabbath all His life and gives no encouragement to those who do not keep it holy. But He has little patience with the multiplied nit-picking rules that have accumulated over the centuries. *"The sabbath was made for man,"* He insists, *"not man for the sabbath"* (Mark 2:27). But He also adds, *"The Son of man is lord even of the sabbath."* We have no right to degrade it.

Hypocrites is a term often hurled at religious leaders. I frequently hear it in my calling. What hurts is that I have to admit the truth, sometimes. When a church is insensitive to human suffering, when worship programs and Bible studies become ends in themselves and hearing and talking take the place of doing the work of God, when systems (or even animals) are more highly valued than persons, we are only acting religious. We are not being real disciples of Christ; we are hypocrites.

To say that persons are important is to imply something else: **persons' bodies are important as well as their souls.** Here Jesus separates himself from much of the teaching of His time. The ancient world often despised the body, agreeing with Epictetus who said that he was a poor soul shackled to a corpse. Some Christians are actually more pagan than Christian in their attitude toward the body. They agree with Epictetus but not Christ, who cared enough about human bodies to take the trouble to heal a great many of them.

William Booth, the founder of the Salvation Army, did not overlook this aspect of Christ's con-

cern. He remembered that Jesus, before feeding the five thousand, said, "*Give ye them to eat*" (Matthew 14:16, *King James Version*), and those words became the inspiration for his starting his Food-for-the-Million shops and his practice of giving men and women free meals.

The always-practical James speaks right to this point: "*If a brother or sister is ill-clad and in lack of daily food, and one of you says to them, 'Go in peace, be warmed and filled,' without giving them the things needed for the body, what does it profit? So faith by itself, if it has no works, is dead*" (2:15-17).

Christians therefore cannot be satisfied to "save souls." The whole person is the object of God's love. A disciple of Christ cannot turn his back on poverty, hunger, or illness. He does not fulfill Jesus' ministry by merely praying for the poor or lost. He ministers with food and medicine as well as with Scriptures and prayer.

Another lesson is inescapable here: By attributing the woman's illness to the power of Satan, Jesus teaches that **physical health is not related only to phsyical causes.** He says, *"Ought not this woman, a daughter of Abraham whom Satan bound for eighteen years, be loosed from this bond on the sabbath day?"* (v. 16).

When Jesus healed the paralyzed man carried to Him by his friends (Mark 2), He approached the man's illness in exactly the same way. *"My son, your sins are forgiven."*

We have trouble grasping Jesus' insight into the sources of suffering. When we take our bent bodies to a physician, we expect him to talk to us about germs or cell structure or nerve damage. Were he to talk about our sins or about some supernatural demonic force we would quickly excuse ourselves and seek a more qualified practitioner.

It is hard for us to realize how *modern* modern medicine really is. We expect doctors to analyze each patient individually, without reference to any universals. Medieval and ancient physicians, on the other hand, often focused on universals and almost ignored the individual. A modern doctor, for example, tries to locate the pain and the specific organ that causes the trouble; in a much earlier age, the doctor would consider the placement of the stars, the family relationships, the man's lifelong diet, the structure of his face, and maybe even the entrails of a newly killed animal. The individual body was part of the total universe and could not be understood apart from the whole.

We would scarcely place any faith in the medieval physician—but many of his patients got well! Perhaps ancient and medieval physicians were as effective as they were in spite of their ignorance of organic causes, because they paid their patients the compliment of seeing them as part of a much larger whole. They knew that physical health was more than a matter of proper diet and exercise and rest; it

59

was—and is—related to family relationships, personal attitudes, and spiritual wholeness.

We don't want to return to those earlier days of medical service. But we should undoubtedly retreat somewhat from today's extreme materialism which ignores the provable fact that more than the body is involved in physical health. Jesus made the woman whole by reaching beyond her fused vertibrae to destroy Satan's hold on her.

Christ's healing touch brings her new joy. *"She praised God"* (v. 13). *"All the people rejoiced at all the glorious things that were done by him."* (v. 17)

The spirit of celebration following her healing is but another indication that praise is at the heart of the Christian faith. *"Rejoice in the Lord always; again I will say, Rejoice,"* the apostle Paul could write from prison (Philippians 4:4), and James begins his letter, *"Count it all joy, my brethren, when you meet various trials,"* assuring his readers that even difficulties eventuate in the Christian's joyful completeness. Jesus and His friends were condemned because they were not appropriately "religious" in the eyes of some (Mark 2:18 ff), but Jesus was unmoved by their criticism. They had judged John the Baptist (saying, *"He has a demon"*) for his ascetic way of life, and Jesus they labeled *"a glutton and a drunkard, a friend of tax collectors and sinners!"* (Matthew 11;16 ff), but Jesus would not alter His course to satisfy His critics. He would bring joy to the people whether His opponents liked it or not.

His gift is a real, not a manufactured, joy. Some years ago I learned of a sales manager of an American store who hired Jay B. Idden, a New York stage director, to teach his salesmen how to smile. The manager had concluded that smiling assistants sold more goods than his nonsmiling ones. So Mr. Idden was employed to take the men one by one, rehearse their smiles, criticize them, and embarrass them until they learned how to smile effectively. He had to give up. The experiment failed. He could teach the mouth to

60

smile (although it must have looked more like a smirk), but he could do nothing about eyes that would not light up. They remained hard and unfriendly; there was no inward joy shining through them.

No one has to instruct the newly healed woman how to smile. She has been released. The Savior does that. He frees men and women from burdens of guilt that bend us over as badly as the woman was bent by her spirit of infirmity. He also frees us from crippling fear of the future. To be free of the past and the future is to celebrate the joy of today, for what is celebration if it isn't a timeless period of utter rejoicing, without worry about yesterday or tomorrow?

In 1977, *Chicago Tribune* Assistant News Editor Charles C. Parvin and his wife celebrated by leaving their home and job in Chicago to serve for a year as missionary volunteers in Korea. The couple in their late forties felt compelled to go as an act of joyful gratitude.

Several years earlier Mrs. Parvin, then thirty and the mother of three children, a dancer and singer with her own studio, fell one morning and was unable to rise. Five months later her rapidly worsening condition was diagnosed as a rare degenerative condition related to muscular dystrophy. The Parvins were told that within a year she would be bedridden and within five years dead.

This went on for fourteen years, while she suffered constant pain, frequent stays in the hospital, and the side effects of the thirty pills a day she had to take. Her weight rose from 120 to two hundred pounds, and her weakened skin tore at the slightest bump. She had two hundred stitches in one of her legs.

To support her, Parvin took the night shift at the *Tribune*, took care of the children by day, and taught high school in the afternoon.

By November 1972 the fight seemed nearly over. The doctors were helpless. But one night—and she insists she was not deluded by drugs—Mrs. Parvin, a

61

devout Christian, said she saw Christ surrounded by light. He told her that she was healed, but that she should tell no one.

Improvement came immediately. Parvin noticed it too, but they didn't dare talk about it for weeks.

When she returned to her doctor, he said, "You must be in a remission, but I've never seen one in this disease before." She informed him that she didn't have the disease anymore. Moreover, her heart damage, her ulcer, and her hernia were also healed. In June 1974 she discarded her wheelchair. She was a new woman.

The Parvins wondered how they could appropriately thank God. Then through the United Presbyterian Church they applied to the Volunteers-In-Mission agency and were sent to South Korea, where they worked in hospitals and Bible studies. While there they supported their youngest child, Scott, as he went through college (with the last of their savings) and also underwrote the cost of high school for three South Koreans.

Their children are now embarked on religious careers.

My reason for telling you their story, however, is to be able to quote the Parvins' summary of what has happened to them. They quietly say, "There's a quality of joy in our lives."[1]

It is the joy of everyone who has been made whole by Jesus Christ.

Footnotes

[1]From *The Washington Post*, reprinted in *The Indianapolis Star* (The Macmillan Company, © July 25, 1977).

Chapter 8

A Two-Time Loser Wins Big

(Luke 17:11-19)

When a thankful Mossi tribesman wishes to express his gratitude, he says, "My head is in the dirt."[1] The words derive from the Mossi custom of showing thanks by bowing low before another and pressing one's head against the earth. For these Africans the proper way to offer thanks is to humble oneself before one's benefactor.

The African custom is not very far removed from the act of this grateful leper whom Jesus has just cured. Actually, ten men were afflicted by the dreaded disease. One of them, a Samaritan, amazed to see his fingers and toes restored, and to sense feeling return to his numbed skin, praised God and fell on his face at Jesus' feet. "My head is in the dirt" he could have said, for so it was.

How can we comprehend the complex of emotions surging through the man? He was a leper in a day when lepers were social losers, outcasts, with little hope of entering human society. They were unclean. Their pitiful condition was carefully prescribed in Leviticus 13:45, 46:

"The leper who has the disease shall wear torn clothes and let the hair of his head hang loose, and he shall cover his upper lip and cry, 'Unclean, unclean.' He shall remain unclean as long as he has the disease; he is unclean; he shall dwell alone in a habitation outside the camp."

The rest of society had to be protected from this cluster of highly infectious diseases called leprosy, of

63

course. Not all of the symptoms of what were called leprosy were chronic or fatal; some so-called lepers recovered, and, after a quarantined period, were returned to normal life. Many, however, did not. Their futures were bleak.

We don't know the precise form of leprosy that had attacked the ten men Jesus cured on this occasion. What we do know is that they were men nobody wanted around, for they were dwelling in the "no-man's-land" along the border between the mutually hostile provinces of Galilee and Samaria. They seem to have been mostly Jews, but at least one of them was a Samaritan. He would normally never have been allowed to associate so freely with the Jews, who held themselves to be morally superior to the Samaritans. In Jesus' day Jews and Samaritans eyed each other with the same suspicion that characterizes Israeli-Palestinian relations today. The Samaritan was, in a very real sense, a two-time loser: first, he was a leper, and, secondly, he was a minority-group member forced by his disease into the unwelcoming company of his traditional enemy.

On the day that Jesus passed through this border village, the small band of lepers waited for Him on the outskirts of the place forbidden to enter. When they spied Him coming they called out to Him, "Jesus, Master, have mercy on us." Word of Jesus' healing ministry had reached them, even in their isolation, and they dared to hope that He would help them. Perhaps they heard how in Galilee, when He had concluded the famous teaching we know as the Sermon on the Mount, a leper had knelt before Him and said, "Lord, if you will, you can make me clean." Jesus defied one of the strongest taboos of the Jews when He reached out and touched the man, who was immediately cleansed.

Emboldened by Jesus' reputation, then, these ten dared to appeal to Him for help also.

Jesus did not touch them or go to them. He almost casually asserted His authority over their disease by sending them to the priest as if they were already whole. Only the priests could pronounce them clean (see Leviticus 14:1-32).

They obeyed immediately. We tend to overlook this fact as we concentrate on the later return of the one leper. All ten believed Him and did precisely what He told them. Had they doubted or disobeyed, the story would have had a different ending, but they didn't. They followed Jesus' orders, and they were healed.

It is impossible not to see the similarities between nine nonreturning lepers and dutiful, obedient Christians who do not hesitate to do what they believe their Lord wants them to do. No one can question their faith. They are regular in worship attendance, they give money, they even hold a job or two in the congregation. But something seems to be missing in their Christian experience. They are dutiful, but not joyful. They accept their share of "church work," but they plod through their routines with a heavy sense of "ought to" and little "want to." Theirs is Christianity of the minimum; they do what must be done, they obey to the letter, but they miss the additional blessing which the returning leper receives. He is the big winner. Albert Schweitzer, commenting on this incident, refuses to charge the others with ingratitude. He believes all ten were grateful but first hurried home to greet friends and take care of their business. Intending to return to thank Jesus later, the press of matters at home prevented them doing so before Jesus was put to death.[2] Schweitzer is probably a little too kind. I may be overly cynical, but the proportions seem about right to me. Only one out of ten—ten percent said thanks. This is true to human nature. Very few persons live lives of genuine thankfulness.

But those who do are the big winners. I recently read Susan Atkins' disturbing autobiography, *Child of Satan, Child of God.* You may recognize her name. She was a member of the Charles Manson family and a participant in the Sharon Tate and La Bianca murders. Susan left her unhappy home and plunged into about every kind of personal sin imaginable: liquor, drugs, sex, theft, murder. She was a bitter, foulmouthed, frightened young woman. But in prison this two-time loser was led to Christ. Her new life is the reverse of everything she was before. She enjoys a new purity of body and language, a new love for those whom she formerly hated, a new beauty in her face and eyes, and, most of all, a new attitude of life based on her gratitude. She had cried, "Jesus, Master, have mercy on me," and He did. Now she constantly gives thanks.

Malcolm Muggeridge, the British writer with poisoned pen, late in life gave himself to Christ. He who formerly could deftly describe every human fault and foible and who made himself miserable by his own diabolical cleverness, now writes of himself, "A sense of how extraordinarily happy I have been, and of enormous gratitude to my creator, overwhelms me often. I believe with a passionate, unshakable conviction that in all circumstances and at all times life is a blessed gift."[3] He, too, in his way, had cried "Have mercy on me" and was saved from himself. Gratitude now marks his life.

Several years ago I was asked to write out my own testimony for a group of college students. It was my first time to share this aspect of my life with my students, so the experience was quite good for me. I must have surprised them, however, when I announced my title, one not at all original but certainly truthful: "Confessions of a Happy Man." In those days (the turbulent 60's) no student with any self-respect would admit to being happy—the cares of the world weighed too heavily upon him to admit such a frivolous attitude. I *was* happy, however, and could only trace my happiness to a sense of God's unfailing goodness to me. I called it happiness. I could have easily—and perhaps more accurately—have called it gratitude.

66

It would be good for you to have to write such a testimony, wouldn't it? You would probably discover, as I did, that there is much in your life to complain about. Undoubtedly your parents did not fully understand you, and they certainly made outrageous mistakes in raising you. Your schools were quite inferior and your childhood filled with legitimate and illegitimate fears. Your boss has been a tyrant, neighbors uncooperative, and the manager of your kids' Little League team doesn't know as much about baseball as you do. Your finances are a mess, your church is full of hypocrites, and your government is destroying the country. On top of all of that the weather has been terrible. True, all true. You certainly have no reason to be grateful.

But what shall we say about these disturbingly joyful people who have been through as much difficulty as you—or maybe more—yet they are so exasperatingly contented? They agree with Muggeridge that life is a blessed gift and they praise God in the same circumstances that drive others to curse Him.

Apparently, gratitude has very little to do with what happens to one and very much to do with what one happens to be. Ten lepers were healed. One said thanks. Jesus was hoping for more. *"Were not ten cleansed? Where are the nine?"*

Among the twentieth century's tragic figures towers that giant of a figure and personality, Lyndon B. Johnson. When he was thrust so suddenly into the presidency by John Kennedy's assassination, he quickly signaled to a waiting America his desperate desire to succeed as the President of all the people. Even more than success he wanted love. He operated in the White House as a benevolent dictator, assuming all the people's problems, dispensing programs and dollars to solve every human ill. Observers of his presidency were pained to see this eager man who earnestly sought his people's love become so hated during the latter days of his tenure in office that he could hardly leave the White House. "How is it pos-

67

sible," he asked in his bewilderment, "that people could be so ungrateful to me after I have given them so much?"

The answer to his question lies deep in the corrupted human heart. How could nine lepers, suddenly set free, forget their Liberator so quickly? Is it possible that the Russian novelist Dostoevski is right in his description of us: "I believe the best definition of man is the ungrateful biped"? Time and time again Shakespeare returned to this theme:

Blow, blow, thou winter wind,
Thou art not so unkind as man's *ingratitude;*

Amiens, *As You Like It*

This was the most unkindest cut of all;
For when the noble Caesar saw him stab,
Ingratitude, more strong than traitors' arms,
Quite vanquish'd him: then burst his mighty heart;

Mark Antony, *Julius Caesar*

How sharper than a serpent's tooth it is
To have a *thankless* child!

King Lear, *King Lear*

I hate ingratitude more in a man,
Than lying, vainness, babbling, drunkenness,
Or any taint of vice. . . .

Viola, *Twelfth Night*

Dietrich Bonhoeffer, so influential in this century, wrote from his Nazi concentration cell, "It's a queer feeling to be so utterly dependent on the help of others, but at least it teaches one to be grateful, a lesson I hope I shall never forget. In normal life we hardly realize how much more we receive than we give, and life cannot be rich without such gratitude.[4]

"Life cannot be rich without such gratitude." That's why I am claiming that the Samaritan, the two-time loser, is a big winner. He has the capacity for a rich life. He receives the extra blessing from the Lord.

He has said thanks. Thanks and praise—did you notice?—are one. *"Then one of them, when he saw that he was healed, turned back, **praising God** . . . giving him **thanks**."* Jesus, accepting the man's

69

thanks, asks, *"Was no one found to return and give praise to God except this foreigner?"*

Other Scriptures equate thanksgiving and God-praising:

"Praise the Lord!
O give thanks to the Lord, for he is good"
(Psalm 106:1)

"Rejoice always, pray constantly,
give thanks in all circumstances;
for this is the will of God in Christ Jesus
for you" (1 Thessalonians 5:16-18)

The simple word of thanks which Jesus offers before breaking bread with His disciples (Matthew 26:27) combines gratitude for the food with praise to God for providing it. To praise is to give thanks.

What we need, then, is to allow George Herbert's famous prayer to become ours:

Thou that hast given so much to me,
Give one thing more—a grateful heart.
Not thankful when it pleases me,
As if thy blessings had spare days,
But such a heart, whose pulse may be thy praise.

Footnotes

[1]Thanks to Roger William Thomas for this information. See his "Lord, Just One Thing More!" *Christianity Today,* November 23, 1973.

[2]*Albert Schweitzer: an Anthology,* ed. Charles R. Joy (Boston: The Beacon Press © 1947, enlarged edition, 1956), p. 152.

[3]*Jesus Rediscovered* (Collins: Fontana Books © 1969), p. 58.

[4]*Letters and Papers From Prison* (Collins: Fontana Books © 1959), p. 28.

Chapter 9

"Do You Want to Be Healed?"

(John 5:1-18)

The man's problem is not only physical. *"Sir, I have no man to put me into the pool when the water is troubled."* I have no one. Loneliness is an anguish worse than physical pain. Contrast this man, if you will, with the paralytic Jesus healed (Mark 2). On that occasion Jesus was teaching in a crowded house in Capernaum when a paralyzed man was brought to Him on a mat carried by four friends. They made an opening in the ceiling and lowered the paralytic to the floor at Jesus' feet so that He could heal the man. It impresses me that even though this patient was very ill, he still had friends who took care of him.

What is so sad about this man at the Bethzatha pool (Bethesda, Bethsaida) is that he has no one to care about him. I wonder why. Is it that he has been sick for so long that people have forgotten him? Oh, we take care of our sick ones—for a while. In the church we're very good with our calling and our caring and our telephoning—at first. But after a while sickness becomes a burden and caring for sick people becomes a bore. So we ignore them! Maybe that is this man's problem. He has been sick for so long that he has been forgotten.

Or perhaps he has an unpleasant personality. It's rather evident that he is somewhat dull. He doesn't even remember to ask who it was that healed him. But then, why shouldn't he be dull? Thirty-eight years he has been there. I've seen them myself—the beggars in India and Mexico and just about everywhere.

71

Day after day the same, lying in the sun, baked by its merciless heat, no one to talk to, no friends. Why shouldn't they be dull?

Here is a man for whom nothing can be done. You know what we do with such people. Eyes clouded with guilt, we turn away from them. After a while, we don't even see at all. So this man has become a man nobody sees anymore. In a society built upon the proposition that it's every man for himself, you walk by, you turn your eyes away from the incurably ill.

Not that he is entirely without hope. Something fascinating happens periodically in this pool. There is a strange bubbling up of the water. One man has suggested that there was a subterranean stream underneath that pool causing the periodic turbulence. We don't really know. The Scripture says that an angel of the Lord would come down at certain seasons to disturb the pool (v. 4). The *Revised Standard Version* does not include this verse, by the way, because it is not in the oldest manuscripts. Since it seems to be a later addition, we don't really know what caused the bubbling, but the people believe that the first one in after the tumbling of the waters will be healed.

But this man can't get there, because no one will help him. So he lies there, year after year after monotonous year, an invalid—and this in Jerusalem, the Holy City, the religious center. Visit the Holy City today and you'll find the same impersonal neglect of persons in the shadows of cathedrals and temples. No help for this man. He has become a man nobody sees.

But throughout His ministry Jesus deliberately sought the tough case, the unwanted man. He had earlier sought out that Samaritan woman whom nobody else of His culture would have dared talked to (John 4). He made a career of looking for the overlooked ones—and He still seeks them through His church today. He knows that our society is organized

72

around the principle of the survival of the fittest. Don't we say (and mistakenly think we are quoting the Bible), "God helps those who help themselves"? But what about those who can't help themselves? We excuse ourselves with these famous words, "Am I my brother's keeper?" We conveniently forget that the words were first spoken by a murderer. Don't we grumble and complain about the welfare system? Yet we critics of our welfare system still must answer this question: What shall we do with those who cannot compete in this competitive society? What will we do with the downtrodden? The outcast? The sick? The maimed? Jesus, in this instance, helps a man nobody else will help. He did it—and so must we.

His question to the man is at first puzzling. *"Do you want to be healed?"* Well, of course he wants to be healed. He's been there for thirty-eight years. Why should the question even be raised? Because, quite simply, many people *don't* want to be healed. Over the years I have dealt with countless persons who prefer sickness to health. When I was teaching high school I was startled one day in the teacher's room when I overheard a conversation. A nonsmoking teacher was chiding one of the smokers for her habit. She said, "You know, you're going to die if you keep it up. Those cigarettes are going to kill you." The smoker's answer? "Well, at least I'll die happy." Then she coughed.

I've counseled with drinkers who don't want to be healed, chronic worriers, workaholics, anxiety-ridden personalities, physically ill people, who don't want to be made whole. Oh, they say they do. But they don't! You may have seen a recent issue of *Newsweek*. The lead article was on pain. One of the doctors interviewed in that article said flatly that the overwhelming majority of chronic pain patients need to have their whole lives examined. Why? Because they're willing to take a pill, or even to be hospitalized to get rid of their pain. But they're not willing to make the necessary changes in their life-styles to be cured. As a result, some doctors guess that eighty to ninety percent of our illnesses have psychological rather than physical causes.

No wonder Jesus asks the man, "Do you want to be healed?" Not everybody does.

He could also be implying, "Have you given up?" Perhaps he has. Thirty-eight years is a long time. He probably has grown accustomed to his lot, preferring the misery of the life that he knows to the risks of a life as a well person.

Or maybe Jesus is asking, "Will you put forth the effort to be healed? Will you try? Do you want to be well enough that you'll try?" We know something about the will to live and the will to get well. Even something as simple as a broken bone, I personally discovered, can be affected by your attitude. But the best example that I have seen, because it came so close to home, was watching my father in the intensive care unit of a Salt Lake City hospital in which he had his open-heart surgery. I've seen it many times before, but it hits a little harder when the patient is your own dad. He had just recovered consciousness. His body was still cold from the lowered temperature. Tubes and wires were running everywhere and the machines were blinking off and on.

I'd forgotten about my brother. As a minister I'm in and out of hospitals all the time, but John had never seen a heart patient immediately following surgery before. He nearly fainted. I should have warned him. I was feeling sorry for him and for dad when the nurses, under orders from the doctor, said to him. "Mr. Lawson, you've got to cough. You've got to keep that fluid out of the lungs. Cough!"

I wanted to yell something at her. The poor man had just recovered his consciousness. He hurt! And now she was demanding that he hurt even more. "Cough!" Did you ever have to cough right after surgery? But he coughed. Hurting all over, he coughed. Why? Because he wanted to get well, that's why. If I'd had my way, I'd have kept him sick. I didn't want him to hurt. I wouldn't have made him cough. But those who knew better said to him, "Mr. Lawson, try! Put forth the effort. *Do you want to get well?*" They knew, as most of us admit when we're honest, that there is very little progress, very little healing, without effort that hurts.

A few years ago there was a revealing article in *Saturday Review* by Editor Norman Cousins. Back in the early '60's he was given one chance out of five hundred to recover from an illness, a collagen disease. In fact, his doctor said he had never seen anyone recover from it. In spite of these overwhelming odds, Cousins decided that he wasn't going to die. He began doing some serious thinking about the relationship between his attitude and his health. Convinced that his pain medicine was retarding his recovery, he threw it away. He hurt. He hurt badly. But he was afraid the medicine might have a toxic effect in his body, so he threw it away. Of this act he said, "I knew that pain could be affected by attitudes. I could stand pain so long as I knew progress was being made in meeting the basic need."[1] So he hurt—and he healed! There's much more to the story, which I don't have room to tell here. But I know that in little pains and in big pains, big things like open-heart surgery or collagen disease or a little thing like a broken arm, you must want to be healed enough to bear the hurt.

This is true in counseling. How many times this counselor has been frustrated because the person who has come to me with a problem doesn't really want to be delivered. He'll say, "Preacher, help me," but he doesn't mean what he says. He won't put forth the emotional and physical effort necessary to cure the problem.

A well-known pastoral counselor in Kentucky says that in his experience with those who come to him for help, one third will improve no matter what he does, another third will never improve no matter what he does, so he's able to help only the remaining third. My figures agree with his.

A good friend of mine and I were talking about healing recently, and Jim suggested that probably the key to all of this is humility, the willingness to bow down before God and those who have the ability to help us and accept their help. Jim is right. Many say they want help and they travel from counselor to counselor and from doctor to doctor crying, "Help me!" But they will not humbly accept the conditions under which they can be helped.

Leslie Weatherhead tells of an incident of a woman who was told in the hospital that she had incurable cancer. It discouraged her somewhat. But the remarkable thing is what happened a little later. The doctor came back in and he said, "I'm sorry, we made a mistake. We misdiagnosed your case. It isn't cancer." Then the woman was desolate. She refused to leave the hospital. She was more upset than ever. She said, "I cannot bear the thought of facing life again."[2] She didn't want to be well.

So we can understand why Jesus has to ask the man, "Do you want to be healed?" Apparently, Jesus senses that the man *does* want to be made well, so He heals him. We notice the words that He uses: *"Rise, take up your pallet, and walk."* And later He says to the man, *"See, you are well! Sin no more."* Here, as elsewhere, Jesus demonstrates the relation between our life-style and our health, our sins and our sicknesses.

Look at those words carefully and hear what Jesus is saying. "Rise," He says to the man, "Rise! Do the impossible! For thirty-eight years you've been lying there on that pallet. You're convinced you can't get up. Now, I'm telling you, get up! do the impossible!"

We must listen to the Lord here. If my God is not the God of the impossible, then what kind of a God is He? I've been to New York City. I've seen the World Trade Building. I know you cannot crawl up the outside of that building to the top of its 110 stories. It's impossible. But somebody did it. More amazing
76

things than this have been done. The blind have seen, the deaf have heard, the paralyzed have walked.

Got any rivers you think are uncrossable?

Got any mountains you can't tunnel through?
God specializes in things thought impossible.

He does the things others cannot do.[3]

Jesus says to the man, "Get up!" Do the impossible!" And then He adds, "Take up your pallet. Don't go back to bed once you're healed. Burn your bridges behind you. Throw away your security blanket. Make a complete departure from your old, inadequate, dependent way of life. Take up your pallet, and walk. Move under your own power. Be a dependent no longer. Sin no more; walk according to the light. Walk!" And the man does what he is told. He is so excited he forgets to say thanks. He forgets to get Jesus' name, so when Jesus' enemies come to find out about this man who dares to break a little rule on the Sabbath he can't tell who has done it.

Isn't this sad? Jesus has just given a man life, and the religious nit-pickers want to kill Him for it. A pitiful commentary on ungodly human nature. It will be sad for us if we neglect the lesson in this passage, sad for the church if we don't understand that we must look for those whom Jesus saw. We must learn the lesson for the Christian that we, too, can live and be whole. We must realize that we share in the church's life-giving ministry.

Here is the argument in a nutshell: those who want a full and complete life will find healing in God. A few years ago, during the American Academy of Medicine meeting in New York, a prominent physician told a group of pastors and doctors that modern medicine had too long concentrated on the study of disease and had not studied the patient well enough. He gave this illustration: A plumber was examined and was found to have a serious heart condition. After reading his EKG and X-rays, the doctors told him he had to give up work immediately and avoid all exertion or he would die. A year later the man was showing great improvement. He was back to doing light work and was planning to return to work full time. The doctor called him in and ran the tests again. The results were remarkable. To the amazement of the doctors, they were unable to discover even the slightest symptom of the disease that had been so prominent just twelve months before.

They asked the man what he had been doing these last twelve months to effect such a change.

He explained that the future didn't look very bright to him. He followed their instructions for a while, but since he had nothing else to do, he began reading his Bible, something he hadn't done for a long time. As he read it, the peace of God came into his life, and, little by little, he noted that he was improving. He has kept up the practice of Bible reading ever since.

The doctor concluded his report by saying, "We discharged the man. He was healed!"[4]

It is my firm conviction that in the church today we are in the healing business. We have the same Bible, the same life-giving God. The Lord who healed the paralytic is still at work. He offers a full and complete life to all who believe in Him, and who are willing to rise and take up their beds and walk in His way.

Footnotes

[1]*Saturday Review*, May 28, 1977.

[2]Quoted in *The Touch of the Master's Hand*, Charles Allen (New York: New Family Library, © by Fleming H. Revell Co., 1956), p. 45.

[3]"Got Any Rivers" © 1945. Renewal 1973 by Oscar C. Eliason. Assigned to Singspiration, Inc. All rights reserved. Used by permission.

[4]John Sutherland Bonnell, *No Escape From Life* (New York: Harper & Bros., 1958), pp. 145, 146.

Chapter 10

"Whoever Lives and Believes in Me Shall Never Die"

(John 11:1-46)

Among the many impudent acts of my youth which I would undo if I could is one that I committed all too frequently in our Sunday evening youth meetings. Our adult advisor often asked us to answer roll call with a verse of Scripture. Several of us fellows, admiring our ingenuity, would race to be first to announce, "Jesus wept." We loved John 11:35 because of its brevity and as long as we had it handy, we didn't have to memorize anything harder.

We thought we were cute. We weren't, of course; we were insensitive and irreverent. There is nothing flippant about Jesus' tears for His friends. They silently testify to His sympathy with people caught in the awfulness of death's grip. The tears demonstrate once again the *compassion of Christ.*

In this, as in so many other ways, Christ reveals the character of God. Greek and Oriental religions had no similar concept of God as a living participant in human struggles. To them God was pure spirituality, aloof from men and unstained by any contact with our impurity. The Jew, on the other hand, had a rich heritage of God's activity on earth. His picturesque vocabulary glistened with images and metaphors of God busying himself in the affairs of His people. To them God was father, mother, nurse, brother, husband, friend, warrior, potter, builder, judge, king, farmer, shepherd, and much, much more.

It is not surprising, then, that the Son who came to reveal the living God to His people should express laughter and love, sadness and sorrow. He was one of us. He did not steel himself against human hurts. He would himself later cry out in pain on the cross. Death would not be taken casually even by the Lord of life.

His mysterious behavior in the raising of Lazarus adds to *our confusion* about healing, however. The disciples' question strikes us as most reasonable: Why did He wait until Lazarus had been in the tomb four days before arriving in Bethany? His critics were right, also. Surely a man who had opened the eyes of the blind man could have prevented Lazarus' death had he wanted to.

Mary and Martha must have been particularly puzzled and certainly disappointed by Jesus. As soon as they became aware of the severity of Lazarus' illness, they sent word to Him. They didn't even bother to request that He come. *"Lord, he whom you love is ill,"* was all they said, but ordinarily the brief message would have been enough to fetch their brother's closest Friend immediately. Jesus always had been eager to help.

But this time He didn't come. The sisters cannot stifle a rebuke when they greet Him. *"Lord, if you had been here, my brother would not have died."* Martha says it first, then Mary. But Martha says even more: *"And even now I know that whatever you ask from God, God will give you."* I wonder what she means. When Jesus tells her that Lazarus will rise again, she thinks He is simply uttering the cliche'that found itself so quickly on the lips of mourners comforting one another. There was a general belief in life after death among most Jews, and Martha accepts Jesus' assurance as a reference to that belief.

Jesus means more, however. He is promising a literal, physical rising from the dead. He is also alluding to His larger purpose, one that they cannot understand until Lazarus has been returned to them. His purpose is to use Lazarus' experience to foreshadow His own resurrection. *"I and the Father are one,"* He has earlier taught His disciples, and they have seen His power over death, but nothing like what they are about to see.

According to rabbinic tradition, which dates in written form from early third century A.D., a soul hovers by the grave for three days in hope of reunion with the body, but at the first sign of decomposition it departs. John therefore draws attention to the four days Lazarus spent in the tomb to emphasize the enormity of Jesus' power. It is important to John to convince his readers that Jesus is Lord (see John 20:30, 31).

The four days give some scholars trouble. They would prefer to believe that Lazarus just swooned (the same argument they will offer to explain Jesus' resurrection). The Lord had earlier raised Jairus' daughter (Mark 5:22 ff) from the dead, but she had been gone so little time her resuscitation does not bother these doubting scholars. Perhaps she, too, was in a swoon. Such an argument can be advanced, if you are so inclined. The same could possibly be suggested for the son of the widow of Nain (Luke 7:11 ff), if you must. But there can be no doubt about Lazarus. There were four days.

We may be confused about Jesus' delay in going to Bethany or about the conditions of His raising Lazarus, but what is in no way confusing is *Christ's power over death and His promise of life.*

"Your brother will rise again." This is not a platitude as Jesus speaks it, but the truth. Look closely at the sequence of events.

First, **the promise:** *"I am the resurrection and the life; he who believes in me, though he die, yet shall he live, and whoever lives and believes in me shall never die."* If Jesus is correct, then even death is not the end. The worst this world can do to us cannot rob us of life.

Then, **the confession.** *"Yes, Lord; I believe that*

you are the Christ, the Son of God, he who is coming into the world." Like most of us in our confession of faith, Martha speaks with complete sincerity, but with incomplete understanding. She believes that Jesus is the Messiah, that in Him God is keeping His promise to send a Rescuer for His people. But she cannot yet comprehend fully what this means. She must await Jesus' next move.

The tears express Jesus' deep feelings for Mary's anguish and the mourning crowd and all death-caused suffering. The quiet statement, "Jesus wept," contrasts starkly with the loud wailing and weeping of the professional mourners, whose cries started with Lazarus' death to continue for seven days. Surrounded by the professionals crying and beating their chests, Jesus stands, His soul aching for Lazarus and his sisters.

The order is as abrupt as it is unexpected. *"Take away the stone."*

Martha's objection betrays the incompleteness of her belief in Christ. She has confessed Him to be Son of God, Christ, the promised one from God. But she is not prepared for what He is about to do. "Lord, he'll smell!" It's too late, she believes. The damage has already been done. Death has won. But Jesus reminds her of their earlier conversation. He will keep His promise.

His prayer is on their behalf, not His own. He has utter confidence in His power and God's steadfastness. Then He discloses his purpose: *". . . that they may believe that thou didst send me."* Now it all makes sense. He did not want to arrive too soon lest there be some other explanation for what He is about to do. He wants no swoon theories, no rationalizing explanations. Once and for all He wants His disciples to believe in His power, especially since He himself will soon be caught in death's clutches.

The invitation to His friend, *"Lazarus, come out"* is spoken by the Lord of life and death. Nothing, even death itself, can resist His power.

"He who lives and believes in me shall never die," He has said. This paradoxical saying admits physical death but assures the believer that there is more. Live in Christ as He is in God, and you, too, can be triumphant over death. Dietrich Bonhoeffer's final words in the Nazi concentration camp are true: "This is the end—for me the beginning of life."

Christ's disciples followed Him throughout His Palestinian ministry, but the real start of their faith was on resurrection morning. When He arose, their faith arose. They did not explain His resurrection as an escape from the grave, the act of a man who swooned temporarily and was revived, nor as a return visit of the Master to His friends, but as an act of the living God in power.

Jesus' power gives us hope. What Christ did for Lazarus, and what God did for Christ also can be done for us.

The famous nineteenth-century American intellectual, Robert Owen, once visited Alexander Campbell to arrange preliminaries for their upcoming debate. As they walked together over Campbell's farm they came upon the family burial plot.

"There is one advantage I have over the Christians," Mr. Owen boasted. "I am not afraid to die. Most Christians have fear in death, but if some few items of my business were settled, I should be perfectly willing to die at any moment."

"Well," replied Campbell, "you say you have no *fear* in death; have you any hope in death?"

"No," he answered after a solemn pause.

"Then," Campbell added, pointing to an ox standing nearby, "You are on a level with that brute. He has fed till he is satisfied, and stands in the shade whisking off the flies, and has neither hope nor fear in death."[1]

For the believer, mourning is no more; hope has filled its place.

Christian history bursts with examples of men and women who have faced death with courage because they believe that "whoever lives and believes in Christ shall never die." Here's a recent instance. An Anglican minister on the Twanda border in Africa was accosted in front of his house by five men who arrived one night in a Jeep. Pastor Yona and a schoolmaster friend—a fellow Christian—were ordered to climb aboard and were driven a short distance away and told to step down near the bank of a river. Knowing that he was about to die, Pastor Yona asked for and received permission to make an entry in his diary.

"We are going to Heaven," he wrote, then noted the time of the night, where certain church funds could be found, and other details. He asked his captors to deliver his diary and the few francs he had with him to his wife.

He and his friend then sang, "There is a happy land . . . where saints in glory stand." One of the rebels took him away, marching him back toward the bridge. As he walked he sang,

There's a land that is fairer than day,
    And by faith we can see it afar;
For the Father waits over the way
    To prepare us a dwelling-place there.

Then they shot him and threw his body into the river.

For some unknown reason, they released his friend and sent him home. The schoolmaster, remarking on the incident later, said of Pastor Yona's murderers, "They were all amazed; they had never seen anyone go singing to his death or walking, as he did, like a man just taking a stroll."[2]

We know how he could do it. He believed Jesus' promise. He walked to his death with hope, for he was looking beyond. His Lord was the Lord of life and death.

William Barclay quotes American Professor Robert McAfee Brown, who was an army chaplain on a troopship returning fifteen hundred marines from Japan to America for discharge. A small group of them asked Brown to conduct a Bible study. He obliged them and, near the end of their voyage, they studied this chapter in John.

"Everything in that chapter is pointing at me," a marine told him. He said he had been in "hell" for the last six months, having gone to Japan straight out of college and into the Marines. In Japan he got himself into deep trouble. Nobody else knew about it, but he did. He was returning to the states as a man who believed his life was ruined. He was dead. "And after reading this chapter," he said, "I have come alive again. I know that this resurrection Jesus was talking about is real here and now, for He has raised me from death to life."[3]

The promises of the Lord of life and death offer His disciples such hope—hope for new life today, hope for a better tomorrow, and after our earth's tomorrows are ended, hope for the day after our tomorrows.

Footnotes

[1]J. Vernon Jacobs, *450 True Stories From Church History* (Grand Rapids: Wm. B. Eerdmanns Publishing Company, 1955), p. 36.

[2]Paul S. Rees, *Don't Sleep Through the Revolution* (Waco: Word Books, © 1969 by World Vision, Inc.), pp. 48, 49.

[3]*The Daily Study Bible: Gospel of John*, Vol. 2 (Philadelphia: Westminster Press, second edition, 1956), p. 119.

Chapter 11

Of Figs and Faith
(Matthew 21:18-22)

This behavior certainly appears to be out of character for Jesus. He was not given to petulance. Cursing the fig tree seems almost like the temper tantrum of a motorist angrily kicking his stalled automobile. Or, if it wasn't temper, it perilously resembles the act of a two-bit magician showing his stuff.

What seems so unusual in Jesus makes sense, however, when this passage is compared with Luke 13:6-9. There Jesus tells a parable of a man who planted a fig tree in his vineyard. After three years the tree still bore no fruit, so he ordered his vinedresser to cut it down. The servant asked for a year's reprieve for the tree, agreeing to remove it if it still was fruitless then. The application of Jesus' parable was obvious to His listeners: a fruitless religion was about to be cut down unless the people repented and began doing God's will.

What Jesus teaches in Luke 13 He acts out in Matthew 21. The cursing of the fig tree is an enacted parable.

It's a **parable of judgment on fruitless religion.** There were leaves on the tree, but no fruit. There was the promise of figs, but no delivery. Jesus viewed His people's religion as promising but not producing. He wasn't the first. Jeremiah had earlier lamented, *"When I would gather them, says the Lord, there are no grapes on the vine, nor figs on the fig tree"* (Jeremiah 8:13). Hosea echoed him, *"Ephraim is stricken, their root is dried up, they shall bear no fruit"* (9:16).

The Jews of Jesus' day could boast of their magnificent temple, their priests proud in their splendor, and their rich heritage of religious traditions. There was the promise of a full life with God—but no delivery.

There was no delivery because what was needed the Jewish faith couldn't give. This same incident is recorded in Mark's Gospel, and Mark adds a fact missing in Matthew's. It was the wrong season for fruit-bearing. *"When he came to it, he found nothing but leaves, for it was not the season for figs"* (Mark 11:13). It was thus incapable of fulfilling Jesus' expectations. Likewise, the popular religion of the Jews could produce leaves of law, temple, priesthood, and Sabbath, but it was helpless to bear the fruits of freedom, peace, and personal salvation as Christians would later come to know them. It, too, would wither in the light of faith in Christ.

This incident is also a **parable of the authority of the Lord.** As Matthew 21 opens, Jesus rides in triumph into Jerusalem to the cheers of the excited crowd: *"Blessed is he who comes in the name of the Lord!"* Into the temple Jesus proceeds, driving out the money changers and perverters of religion, assuming an authority higher than that of the temple bosses who have allowed the people to be defrauded in the name of religion. Out to the suburbs He retreats, where He demonstrates His authority over nature in His cursing of the fig tree, as He has much earlier evidenced His power in calming the angry sea.

There can be no question about it. Even though the chief priests and elders will later ask Jesus, *"By what authority are you doing these things?"* it is clear that He needs no delegated authority—He is the authority!

Primarily, however, His treatment of the fig tree is a **parable of the power of faith.** His disciples want to know how the tree withered at once. Jesus doesn't answer them. He has little patience for explaining His actions; He just asserts His authority. Then He goes

88

even further. "What you have seen me do," He suggests to them, "you can do—and even greater things you can do—if you have faith." What startling words. *"Even if you say to this mountain, 'Be taken up and cast into the sea,' it will be done."*

Jesus never moved a mountain himself, of course. He was not interested in rearranging the terrain. What He did was better than mountain-moving. He restored health to the sick, revealed truth to the confused, returned from the grave when His closest friends thought Him gone forever, opened the doors of Heaven for all who would follow Him, and He granted His believers miracle-working faith.

But look closely. He's talking about a specific kind of faith—one that is prayerful and fruit-bearing.

"If you have faith—" does not refer to the belief of the Sunday-school boy who defined the word for his teacher in this way: "Faith is believing what you know isn't so."

Nor is faith the exercise of the student who prayed on the night before his examination that God would help him pass. He had been taught Jesus' words in John 14:13: *"Whatever you ask in my name, I will do it."* He really wanted to pass the exam, so he prayed—and failed. He nearly lost his faith. The next year he studied harder and passed. Leslie Weatherhead, to whom this happened, learned through the experience that the promise of Jesus, which sounds too good to be true when taken by itself, is really not good enough to be true.

"Prayer would be like putting a coin in the slot and pulling out the bar of chocolate," he concludes. God couldn't run His universe in such a fashion. "Prayer for a quiet mind in the examination would have been answered. Prayer for the magical supply of knoweldge I had not acquired and skill that I did not possess—prayer for an unethical advantage over other boys—was denied."[1]

What kind of faith is Jesus referring to, then? Perhaps we can answer the question indirectly. In the

89

early 1950's, Edward R. Murrow published his famous little volume on faith, *This I Believe*. One of the contributors was the English poet, C. Day Lewis, who correctly reduces faith to its essence, definiing it as "the thing at the core of you, the sediment that's left when hopes and illusions are drained away." More than that, it elicits from you "any sacrifice because without it you would be nothing—a mere walking shadow." As a writer, Lewis has found his own core. "I would," he insists, "sacrifice any human relationship, any way of living to the search for truth which produces my poem."[2]

A strong statement, but faith is just that bold. If you believe in Christ, more than in anything else; if you want to do God's will, more than anything else; then ask in prayer, ask to produce fruit for God—more than anything else—and it will be done.

Hudson Taylor, the famous nineteenth-century missionary to China, helps us to understand this living faith. When he was thirty-three, Taylor felt compelled to penetrate beyond the coastal cities of China into the provinces where millions of people lived without Christ. While he was on a holiday at the seashore, exhausted and nearly ill, he wrote in his journal, "If God gives us a band of men for inland China and they go, and all die of starvation, they will only be taken straight to heaven; and if only one heathen soul is saved, would it not be well worth while?" (Remember C. Day Lewis: "I would in the last resort sacrifice any human relationship . . . ''?)

So he decided to gamble everything for God. He wrote on a leaf in his Bible: "Prayed for twenty-four willing, skillful workers at Brighton, June 25, 1865." Then he added, "If we are obeying the Lord, the responsibility rests with Him, not with us!"

Taylor was obeying the Lord and the Lord responded magnificently. He received an unsolicited fifty dollars. In the next century, that first gift would be followed by thirty-six million, all unsolicited. More than three thousand missionaries responded to
90

China's call. Taylor "moved mountains," because he really asked in prayer and faith.[3]

One morning during our worship services I became suddenly aware that somebody in our church has been praying fervently. There in the congregation that day were Phil Banta, missionary to Colombia, South America; Mickey Smith, missionary to Indonesia; Tony Calvert, missionary recruit to England; Eric Duggins, missionary recruit to Mexico; and Ron Miller, missionary to prisons. All these men and their equally dedicated wives have recently been sent out from our church. In addition, with us that morning were two intern ministers, preparing for ministerial service, and several other young men and women there and away at college preparing for the ministry. Somebody has been praying. Mountains are being moved.

There are some things that we can't do, of course, and some answers God will not give. He doesn't always answer our wishes. I could wish to be in Australia right now, but the wish doesn't come true. I could wish tomorrow would never come, or that my team would have an undefeated season, or that I were tall.

Some desires are more serious. A very good friend of mine is an orthopedic surgeon. His mother is currently extremely ill with cancer. Her prognosis is not good. Her son, a devout Christian, recognizes that she has gone beyond modern medicine's ability to restore her health. He wishes she would regain her health; he prays for her daily. But he is prepared for the consequences, whatever the answer. He knows from many years of dedicated prayers that God doesn't always restore the sick to health; He does not prevent Christians from dying.

God's answers are in keeping with His character and His plans for the universe; they do not always satisfy our longings. But if we ask prayerfully for fruit in our lives, we shall receive.

This is, finally, a **parable of the danger of fruit-**

91

lessness. A faithless, fruitless tree withers. So does a faithless, fruitless life.

The disciples are standing around Jesus as He deals with the tree. Then He applies His action to them. "You can do this," He tells them. What He doesn't say, but implies by His action, is that you will wither also, unless you bear fruit.

It certainly happens to churches. I am thinking of a church whose life I have observed for thirty years. It is currently but a shell of its former self. It meets in a fine building, but the congregation has shriveled to less than half of its earlier membership. Its vitality is gone. Several years ago the church turned inward, began stressing the "purity" and spirituality of the members. It became critical of other churches. Year after year members left, seeking a more accepting and loving spirit. They wanted to bear the fruit of the Spirit and felt stifled in the judgmental atmosphere of the church.

It happens to persons. On a recent trip I visited with a woman who has passed into her retirement years. She has no outside interests and consequently very little to talk about. She will hardly venture out of her house. Her days are spent in waiting for the end. She has withered. I met another woman, now in her forties. She has already grown old and frightened. Her best years are behind her, she is convinced. She reminisces far too much for such a young woman. There is nothing to which she can give herself enthusiastically.

On the same trip I read Robert Ringer's infamous book, *Looking Out for Number One*. If ever there was a philosophy of life guaranteed to make a person miserable and hasten the withering of the soul, this is it. Although Ringer nods in the direction of doing something for others, it is evident that he does not really believe in living primarily to bear fruit for anyone but oneself. He believes, frankly, in selfishness. He does not teach fruit-bearing. He proclaims the doctrine of withering.

When I visited with Dr. Donald McGavran of the School of World Mission in Pasadena, on the other hand, I met a mountain-moving man. He was over eighty at the time of our visit, but he hardly had time to see me, because he was leaving immediately for India on another fact-finding and missionary-encouraging jaunt. Having given his preretirement years to energetic mission work in India, Dr. McGavran has since retirement age authored several books, established and edited a periodical, started and moved and deaned a graduate school, and is still writing, speaking, teaching, traveling, and inspiring others. Fruit-bearing.

Why hasn't he taken to his rocking chair and television set? Most people his age have done so. He hasn't because he knows that to do so is to wither, and at eighty he is not ready to dry up.

Andrew Blackwood says that three things are essential for spiritual health: food, fresh air, and exer

93

cise. "In the Christian life we think of food as it is found chiefly in the Bible; of fresh air as it comes best on the mountaintop, where a man communes with his Lord; and of exercise as it comes through Christian service down in the valley." Study, prayer, and service—the way to faithfulness and fruitfulness.[4]

Walt Disney, no theologian of course, nevertheless comes close to the meaning of Jesus' enacted parable when he says that "a prayer implies a promise as well as a request." To ask in faith is to promise to do my part, to bear fruit. A religion . . . a church . . . a person that only promises, but doesn't deliver, will die. Therefore, *"have faith and never doubt."*

Footnotes

[1]*When the Lamp Flickers* (Nashville: Abingdon-Cokesbury Press © 1948 by Pierce and Smith), p. 139.

[2]*This I Believe* (New York: Simon and Schuster, Inc. © 1952), p. 101.

[3]From Paul S. Rees, *Don't Sleep Through the Revolution* (Waco, London: Word Books, © 1969), pp. 124, 125.

[4]*Pastoral Work* (Grand Rapids: Baker Book House, 1971, © 1945 by the Westminster Press), p. 226.

Chapter 12

It's Friday— Sunday's Coming

(John 20:1-18)

I wish I could have listened to one of the finest Easter sermons that I've ever heard about. It was a sermon by an old black preacher. Anthony Campolo, an outstanding speaker and sociologist who was also the older man's white associate minister, delighted an Ozark Bible College audience as he boasted about that old preacher's sermon. It was evident that he was proud to be associated with such a man. His sermon was very simple. About all he said was, "It's Friday, Sunday's coming." But of course, he preached for forty-five minutes to a congregation that was not as subdued as the one I preach to, and they entered into the enthusiasm and excitement of that sermon in a way that—well, it could make me a little bit jealous. Powerful sermon. By the time you say, "It's Friday, Sunday's coming," you've summarized the gospel. Simple, but profound.

It's Friday. Friday is the day on which for thirty pieces of silver Judas sells his Master. But Sunday's coming.

It's Friday. Friday is the day on which Peter, who never thought he would do it, denies Christ three times, swearing that he has never even heard of Him. But Sunday's coming.

It's Friday, and the soldiers make a crown of thorns. They mock Jesus and they spit on Him and they do all they can to humiliate Him. But Sunday's coming.

It's Friday, and a mob has been assembled and

primed to lie for the religious leaders. They shout for Barabbas. And of Jesus they cry, *"Let him be crucified."* Friday—but Sunday's coming.

It's Friday, and the Roman governor, splendid in the robes of royalty, calls for a basin. He dips his fingers into the bowl, trying to wash away his guilt in this travesty of justice. He does this on Friday, but Sunday's coming.

Friday is the day that men make, the day when Satan has his way. Because it's Friday in the garden a voice cries out, *"My Father, if it be possible, let this cup pass from me."* In the darkness of Friday, that same voice cries out again, *"My God, my God, why hast thou forsaken me?"* That is Friday—but Sunday's coming.

We are good at Fridays. We can carve a niche in the hillside. We can dig a hole in the ground. We are experts at making graves. We know how to fashion a cross. We bury the dead with proper ceremony. Our workers can seal a tomb. We know how to kill the good. We can make Fridays. But only God can give us a Sunday—and Sunday's coming.

When Mary goes to the tomb with her friends to see Jesus, she is all wrapped up in the Friday spirit. She doesn't know about Sunday. Even when she approaches the empty tomb and she sees the angels, she cannot imagine a resurrection. She naturally thinks somebody has stolen the corpse. So immersed is she in Friday that when she looks at Jesus, she doesn't really see Him. She thinks He is the gardener. To Mary, death is final. She believes the One to whom she has given her life is gone forever.

We have an advantage over Mary. We know that even though Friday seems victorious, Sunday's coming. We may sometimes be discouraged or downhearted, but we can never be defeated, because Sunday's coming.

For a long time I have been a fan of one of our Presidents, Woodrow Wilson. I admire what he attempted for world peace, even though he failed in the attempt. Toward the end of his life was one of his finest moments. It came on the day that the Senate finally and forever defeated Wilson's plan to put the United States into the League of Nations. By this time, Wilson was a very sick man. In traveling throughout the country on behalf of the League he had suffered a paralytic stroke. He was taken back to the White House, and for many weeks this country virtually had no leader. On the day that he was defeated by the Senate, word was brought to the ailing, paralyzed, barely functioning President. It was the Friday of his life. Late into the night he couldn't sleep. Along about three in the morning, his doctor, who had been looking in on him every hour, heard him say, "Doctor, the devil's a busy man." Wilson was quiet for quite a long time.

Then he spoke again. "Doctor, please get the Bible there, and read from 2 Corinthians, chapter 4, verses 8 and 9." The physician got the Bible, opened it, and read aloud to President Wilson these words: *"We are troubled on every side, yet not distressed; we are perplexed, but not in despair; persecuted, but not forsaken; cast down, but not destroyed"* (King James Version). In the Friday of his life, he knew that Sunday was coming.[1]

I wonder whether the doctor read any further? Had he done so, he would have read these words:

"For which cause we faint not; but though our outward man perish, yet the inward man is renewed day by day. For our light affliction, which is but for a moment, worketh for us a far more exceeding and eternal weight of glory; while we look not at the things which are seen, but at the things which are not seen: for the things which are seen are temporal; but the things which are not seen are eternal" (2 Corinthians 4:16-18, *King James Version*).

Oh, it may be Friday—but Sunday's coming!

During World War II, a soldier wrote from the front lines to his former philosophy professor, a Christian. He related to his professor the anguish he had been suffering in the war. He was exhausted from marching and weak from hunger; he was plagued with lice and scratching. The biting cold tormented him. He was barely hanging on to his sanity, and he wrote to his professor that he had not only forgotten the philosophers that he had studied and the other authors that he had read in school, but he added that he was even too weak to leaf through the Bible. His whole spiritual life had become disorganized. "I just vegetate," he concluded.

The professor wrote immediately to encourage him, to be thankful that the gospel is more than a philosophy. "If it were only a philosophy, you would just have it as long as you have your mind and it could afford you very little intellectual comfort. But even when you can no longer even think about God, he still thinks about you."[2] That's the difference between Friday and Sunday.

There are times in the Fridays of our lives when we can't even think about God. Or if we think about Him, we think about Him in the anguish of Jesus on the cross, "My God, my God, where are You? Why have You forsaken me?" Do you ever have moments in your life when you wonder where God is? When it's Friday? The message of Sunday is that even when you think God has forgotten you, He hasn't, and even when you've turned your back on God and you're sinking in discouragement or self-pity, He hasn't forgotten you—and Sunday's coming!

Several years ago a pastor called at a house where there were several children. The parents had never allowed those children to come to Sunday school. The pastor knocked on the door and a little boy opened the door and said, "Hi, Mister." The pastor said, "Hi, Jimmy. I came to invite you to our Sunday school. I'm the preacher." The little boy turned around and yelled, "Hey, Mom, what's a preacher?"

The call paid off and Jimmy was allowed to go to Sunday school, and he went faithfully. But one Sunday he was absent. A little later, two days before Christmas, the minister received a phone call at five in the morning. The voice on the other end said, "I'm Jimmy's mother. Come quickly to the hospital! Jimmy has pneumonia!" By the time the minister got there, Jimmy was gone. The distraught parents buried Jimmy on a hillside as the snow was falling. After the funeral the pastor went to Jimmy's home and he saw the Christmas tree, and he saw the boxes that had been intended for Jimmy. He wondered whether Christmas would ever again come to that family. It was their Friday.

In the month of April, Jimmy's mother and father came before the church to receive Jesus Christ as their Lord and Savior and to give themselves to Him. Following the services, they and the minister went out to the grave and knelt and prayed and thanked God for Sunday. What had happened in that home? They had

99

lost somebody they loved. They thought he was gone. But the pastor was able to show the parents from the Word of God that after Friday—Sunday's coming![3]

And he taught them that even though all their lives they had ignored God, He had not ignored them. He explained that the reason Jesus came and died on the cross was so that we might live. The meaning of the resurrection of Jesus Christ is that the gates of Heaven could be opened for others who also want to come in. For those who are in Christ, death is not a period—it is a comma in a living sentence that lives beyond the grave. There is life after death.

Jimmy's parents told the pastor they wanted that life. After the long winter comes spring and the resurrection of the flowers. And after the long, hard winters of our souls, the Fridays of our lives, comes Sunday.

When Jesus reveals His identity to Mary, He instructs her to deliver His message to His other followers, telling them, *"I am ascending to* **my** *Father and*

your Father, to *my* God and *your* God." The implication is clear: the God who raised Jesus from the dead is also our God; the one He calls Father is Father to us as well. He who seemed to abandon Jesus on that awful night in Gethsemane had not forgotten Him after all; neither will He turn his back on us in the dark nights of our souls. We do not have to be afraid. For us it is true as it was for Jesus: Sunday's coming.

This, then, is the gospel.

It's Friday. Christ is dead. The disciples are scattered. The devil is triumphant. Darkness is everywhere. But Sunday's coming! Sunday *has* come! And we celebrate, not death, but the triumph of life over death; not evil, but the triumph of good over evil; not Satan, but the triumph of God over all the forces that Satan can muster.

Sunday has come!

Footnotes

[1]Gene Smith, *When the Cheering Stopped* (New York: William Morrow and Company, 1964), p. 150.

[2]Helmut Thielicke, *How To Believe Again* (Philadelphia, Fortress Press © 1972), p. 34.

[3]A. K. Thomas, "Enchanted Dust," *Christianity Today*, April 13, 1962.

Chapter 13

Loose in the World
(Luke 24:44-53; Acts 1:1-11)

In John Masefield's poetic drama, *The Trial of Jesus,* Pilate's wife Procula is brooding over the crucifixion of Christ when Longinus, a Roman soldier, comes in to report that he has discovered the tomb of Jesus empty. With great agitation Procula asks Longinus whether he believes Christ's claim that He would rise again.

At first Longinus hedges, saying that anyone who believes something strongly enough to die on a cross for it will find others who will also believe it. Procula will not be put off, however, and again asks whether he believes it. Then Longinus describes Christ as a fine young fellow who singlehandedly defied all the Jews and Romans, but the seasoned soldier really doesn't commit himself.

To her insistent attempt to find out whether Longinus thinks Jesus dead he replies very simply, "No, lady, I don't."

"Then where is he?" she asks him.

"Loose in the world, lady," Longinus answers her, "where neither Jew nor Roman can stop his truth."[1]

Longinus and the author of the Gospel and Acts have come to the same conclusion. Jesus suffered and died and was buried, Luke reports, but also arose from the dead and is now loose in the world through the power of His Spirit. As far as Luke is concerned, then, the miracles haven't stopped.

The supreme miracle, Jesus' resurrection from the dead, is the central affirmation of the Christian church. The preaching of the gospel is not a recital of

Jesus' many miracles, nor a review of His astounding teachings. It is not even an invitation to join the richest fellowship on earth. The gospel, Paul affirms in 1 Corinthians 15:3-5, is this: *"that Christ died for our sins in accordance with the scriptures, that he was buried, that he was raised on the third day in accordance with the scriptures, and that he appeared to Cephas, then to the twelve."*

This is the great fact of the church: that God entered into history in Christ, living in time, loving earth's people, escaping death's grip and defeating the power of Satan, finally leaving the earth—but not entirely leaving, either. He remains loose in the world through His Spirit.

The disciples believed, when they saw the stone rolled into the opening of Jesus' tomb, that the miracles were over. But they were wrong. Mary saw Him alive again; so did Peter and the other apostles—including doubting Thomas. So, Paul says, did more than five hundred, most of whom were still alive when he wrote the 1 Corinthian letter (15:6). Even Paul, who had not met Jesus during His ministry, met the risen Christ (15:8; Acts 9).

Luke describes Jesus' final departure. Having taken His disciples out of Jerusalem to Bethany He blessed them (Luke 24:50) and charged them to stay in Jerusalem until they received the power of the Holy Spirit (Acts 1:8). Then, even as they were watching, He was taken up, and a cloud covered Him as He ascended away from them.

Still the miracles would not be over. Two men appeared to reassure the disciples with the promise that Jesus would miraculously come again.

These passages promise a two-fold miracle, then. Jesus would go away and leave them, but not alone and not forever. His presence would be with them from the moment the Holy Spirit would descend to them on the Day of Pentecost. Then one day, in a remarkable second coming, Jesus would return to claim His own.

In the meantime, He is loose in the world.

Jesus promised the disciples that He would send the Spirit. He kept His promise: His Spirit is with us now.

"And behold," Jesus said, *"I send the promise of my Father upon you"* (Luke 24:49). *"You shall be baptized with the Holy Spirit,"* and, *"You shall receive power when the Holy Spirit has come upon you"* (Acts 1:5, 8).

When the disciples realized that Jesus had conquered death, all their hopes and dreams were revived. At long last, they thought, Israel could finally be set free. They wanted nothing from Jesus more than His restoring the kingdom to Israel. Once again they hoped that Jesus could be the political reformer that many of them had anticipated. They had grown weary of the yoke of Roman authority; they yearned for the day when Israel's people would walk in freedom. If Jesus could now give Israel that independence, all the nation would rejoice—but especially the disciples, because Jesus would undoubtedly make them ministers and authorities in His new Jewish government. No wonder they pressed Him to set Israel free.

But Jesus had better things in store for them. He would found a new nation, supported by a new power, but it would not be what they had in mind. Moreover, they would have to wait for it: *"Stay in the city until you are clothed with power from on high"* (Luke 24:49). These must have been hard words for impatient men to hear.

They had to wait, however, because the task which Jesus was laying upon them—to carry His message to the entire known world—would be impossible to accomplish without the help of the Holy Spirit. It was too big a venture to try alone.

It is not easy for Jesus' followers to wait for God's time. I just received a newsletter from John and Marilyn Mulkey explaining their delay in leaving the United States on schedule for mission work in Indonesia. Someone buried in an office somewhere deep in that country's bureaucratic maze is inexplicably delaying their visa approval. So they remain in their temporary quarters in Hawaii, frustrated at the long delay after so many years of preparation. John writes:

> In our last newsletter I mentioned we hoped that by the time we wrote another newsletter we'd be able to tell you of the granting of our visas. Well, we have not received confirmation yet. I know the feeling you probably have upon reading that last sentence. It's the same drop in emotions we feel each day when the mailman drives off with no new news from Indonesia.
>
> While preparing for missionary service over the last seven years, I read about great men of God like Hudson Taylor in China who longed for the manpower and Godpower to win the people there to Christ who were "dying, a million a month without Christ." It impressed on me the urgency of the task of world mission. And our friends say to us as we wait, 'God's timing is best.' I know they are right, but it still hurts to realize the world need, see our readiness, and yet feel helpless in getting started.

The Mulkeys' feeling of helplessness is not unfamiliar to anyone who has received Christ's instruction to serve Him—but first to *wait*. In my ministry I have repeatedly turned to the passage we are studying. Patience does not come easy for me. I want power now, on my terms, so that I can get to work. I even pray, "Lord, give me patience—but hurry."

Jesus specifically instructed His disciples to wait, however. He wanted them to live in, walk in, and speak through the power of the Spirit. He would not be impressed by their ingenuity, their cleverly constructed plans to expand His kingdom, or their amazing output of energy. He had miracles in mind, and miracles take Holy Spirit power.

Luke makes the task that Christ gave His disciples very plain: They were to preach *"repentance and forgiveness of sins"* in Christ's name (Luke 24:47). They already knew that *"God so loved the world that*

107

he gave his only Son, that whoever believes in him should not perish but have eternal life" (John 3:16). But God's saving work in Christ would be meaningless without somebody publishing the news of salvation. That's why Jesus trained twelve men and established a church—to broadcast the saving message far and wide.

They were to preach repentance. John the Baptist had announced this same theme (Matthew 3:1) and Christ began His ministry with the identical words (Matthew 4:17). Obviously it is essential to one's entrance into Christ's kingdom. To repent is to turn around, to give up old ways for new, to turn from pursuit of the ungodly to pursuit of God's truth. Men and women who are comfortable with things as they are need to be challenged to work for things as they can be.

In a real sense, then, Jesus is instructing His disciples to be revolutionaries. Their mission is to overthrow darkness in behalf of light, to free people from bondage into liberty, to offer them innocence in place of their guilt, to lead them to life out of death. Their message of hope in Christ is not a change of one nation's political leadership, but new life in Christ for all nations.

And new life is what people are seeking. I recently bought gas for my car in a service station run by a young man, probably in his early twenties. He was dirty and unkempt, wearing a T-shirt on which was stamped a picture of a fat, slovenly drunk. The words printed above the derelict were, "Booze is the only answer." I'm sure it was meant to be funny, but I couldn't laugh. I know too many drunks. Unable to cope with the pressures of daily living, they have sought an escape in drink. They want a new life, but they have found death instead. They have succumbed to the temptation to take an easy way out. They have given up.

Destructive temptations lie all about us. Some of our church members recently returned from Las

Vegas. They had never been there before, and they are not gamblers, but they did experiment a bit with the slot machines. Upon their return, they had great fun recounting their experience and explaining how the slot machines work. These "one-armed bandits" are cleverly programmed to pay off early, our new experts taught us, so that players are suckered into putting more and more of their money into the slot in hope of larger and larger winnings. Naturally the machines are designed so that the house always wins more than it pays. There is no way for the customers to come out ahead. Before they realize it, the victims have succumbed to temptation, lost their money, and are in danger of losing everything else. They are betting on something that can never make them winners. They need to be turned around before it's too late in order to be saved from bankruptcy.

That's repentance: to be sorry enough to turn around in order to be saved. Repentance is turning from the damaging allurements of this world's temptations to the saving grace of God. It is letting God rescue us from drink or gambling or selfishness or anything else that keeps us from His saving love. It is turning toward God—and meaning it.

But someone will be sure to say, with a little more arrogance than sincerity, "How can I turn to God? I have gone too far. I have offended Him by my careless life. There's no hope for as great an offender as I am."

Now we are ready for the rest of the message Jesus' disciples are charged to preach: Forgiveness. It is not too late to be forgiven. You haven't gone too far, if you are still willing to turn toward God and let Him have his way with you.

If you need evidence, consider Peter. When Peter stood before the assembled crowd on the Day of Pentecost (Acts 2) to preach the first gospel sermon, his presence there was living proof of the grace of God and the forgiveness of Christ. Only days before he had disgraced himself by publicly denying that he had ever known Jesus. He had allowed his Lord to die as a common criminal without raising his voice to defend Him or protest the treatment He was receiving. Yet Christ forgave him and placed him foremost among the apostles.

If you need more evidence, consider Tex Watson, killer of Sharon Tate and several others when he was a member of Charles Manson's infamous family. Tex is now a forgiven Christian, working as a prisoner to bring other inmates to Christ. For that matter, consider Nixon's "hatchet man," Charles Colson, now devoting all his energy to bringing new life to inmates behind bars. It is impossible to go so far in sin that you are outside the grasp of God's forgiving love, if you will only genuinely repent and ask for that forgiveness.

You see, Christ is still loose in the world, still miraculously changing soiled, sinful lives into cleansed, pure personalities. Through the preaching of the gospel men and women everywhere are currently—that means right now, today—receiving forgiveness for their sins and being granted the gift of the Holy Spirit.

The miraculous power that stilled the angry seas,
    that restored a blind man's sight,
        that cured a leper's curse,
            that made a lame man walk;
The power that awakened Lazarus from the dead,
    that multiplied the fishes and loaves,
        that withered a fruitless tree,
            and cast away the demon's curse;
That power,
    Christ's power,
        miraculous power—
            is loose in the world.
He is changing lives daily.

And He is coming again one day to claim His own. *"This Jesus, who was taken up from you into heaven, will come in the same way as you saw him go into heaven"* (Acts 1:11).

110

But when? How can we know when He is coming, so that we can be certain to be ready? We don't know, so *"you also must be ready; for the Son of man is coming at an hour you do not expect"* (Matthew 24:44).

Another great miracle is coming.

May we all be ready!

Footnotes

[1]John Masefield, *The Trial of Jesus* (© The MacMillan Company).